My best wishes and much love
to Sadie

Regina Engelhardt

To: Sadie,

Merry Christmas

Love you,

From

2021

THAT'S NOT A
Scar;
THAT'S A *Beauty*
Mark

A SPIRITUAL AND INSPIRATIONAL MEMOIR

REGINA ENGELHARDT

BALBOA.
PRESS

A DIVISION OF HAY HOUSE

Balboa Press books may be ordered through booksellers or by contacting:

Balboa Press
A Division of Hay House
1663 Liberty Drive
Bloomington, IN 47403
www.balboapress.com
1 (877) 407-4847

Print information available on the last page.

ISBN: 978-1-5043-4041-0 (sc)
ISBN: 978-1-5043-4043-4 (hc)
ISBN: 978-1-5043-4042-7 (e)

Library of Congress Control Number: 2015914446

Balboa Press rev. date: 01/22/2016

PREFACE

W hen I was fourteen years old, I forgot how to cry. My tears became frozen, stuck somewhere in a time and place so horrible, a memory so unspeakable, that they could not be released. I had images in my mind of endless night raids and angry rebels with rifles. The rebels taunted us, pointed their weapons and forced us into hiding. I actually witnessed their violence — the bodies strewn across land that was once a warm blanket of green grass and wild, sweet blueberries. When I saw them, I realized that those bodies with stiff limbs outstretched helplessly were my neighbors, and I knew that I was observing agony and senseless killings. And, all of it terrified me. I had never known suffering like this before. It was as if the entire world had collapsed around me and I didn't know why. At that point, I realized that hollowness was filling the spaces where tears should have been. I could not weep.

The terror I experienced haunted me for years. That is why I had to write about it. I had to face and spill out a pain that threatened my inner peace and attempted to chip away at my happiness. You see, despite the challenges of my past, I had managed to move forward and get a grip on this thing called joy. Yet, joy is an elusive butterfly. Just when you think you've grasped it, it slips away oh so silently, and you watch in dismay as its fragile wings flap … and it hovers at a distance. But I never gave up. I kept trying, succeeding in some instances and in others, running into walls.

This book is my confession. I have no one to blame for the choices I have made. My only hope is that young people who read this will learn and benefit from my victories and my mistakes. Life can be a bumpy road. We must be on-guard at all times, just like balancing on a wire. The lessons gained along the way are very expensive. But we don't pay for all of them with money. Often, the price we pay is life itself.

Everybody will stumble through or rise above obstacles. My advice (especially to young people) is simply this: Read the lessons that appear at the beginning of each chapter and in between the experiences throughout the book. These lessons are messages from my heart. You could call them my offspring because they are the result of a vision and understanding that took me many years to cultivate. And as you read, remember to always apply the wisdom of elders like me. I want you to learn from my journey. Live freely, but step carefully. There is no end to knowledge. Make your search for it a life-long quest.

On this earth, we all are students and teachers.

Regina Engelhardt

CHAPTER 1

GOD SPEAKS THROUGH NATURE

Lesson: Seeds are planted in dark places. That's where they get strong, take root, and build the foundation to pull themselves into the light.

E very spring delicate buds would sprout on the skinny birch trees lining the streets of Kiwerce. I remember them vividly. Long and slender, they dangled in the wind like leafy caterpillars. They were beautiful to me. I loved nature, even as a child.

In the evening, my friends and I used to sit on our steps, watching the light from the sunset shimmering on the leaves and listening to the swoosh — the gentle sound of the woods shivering and praying. We would actually say, "Listen, the woods are praying." It was almost a sacred ritual for us, huddled together, eavesdropping on the whisperings of branches and leaves. In the summer, we slept with open windows so we'd awaken to the chatter of birds and the musical moans of the frogs. It was like a serenade, inviting us to jump out of bed and get on with another wonderful day.

Before I turned ten, not much else happened in Kiwerce, a small town in southeast Poland near Luck (pronounced Ludsk), the capital of Wolin. My brother, Mitchell, and I were born during what one might consider the best years of that region, and our early childhood could be described as idyllic. Our house was in the suburbs outside of town in a scenic wooded area with a lot of open spaces. Behind our property was a river, so we could swim in the summer and skate in the winter. In the spring and autumn, we would scamper through the woods, gathering blueberries, mushrooms, hazelnuts, and strawberries. We reaped a lot of pleasure picking and eating that good organic, fresh food. At the same time, we saved money. Life was good. When I look back, I do not even remember any severe weather, like floods or destructive storms. The climate in eastern Poland is much like that in Northern Michigan. But back then, it seemed that even the heavens and the earth were kind to us.

We lived in peace with our neighbors, who were Polish, Russian, Ukrainian, and Jewish. Everyone respected each other. Everyone celebrated life. Poland was free for twenty years before World War II, and our economy was doing very well. We had very talented neighbors. One of them was a seamstress, Helena Swierk. I called her Aunt Helena. She made beautiful original dresses for me and my mother. She was very busy because people would dress up to go shopping or go to church. She often had material leftover, sometimes enough to make a dress for me, and so she did. I wore her dresses to school, and my classmates would admire them. Aunt Helena had two daughters a few years older than me, so I also was lucky enough to inherit some of their beautiful dresses. We were very grateful to have them as our neighbors.

The children in our neighborhood all played together and celebrated holidays together. Across the road from our home was a cemetery. Every All Saints Day people lit candles to put on the graves. I used to enjoy the candles so much that sometimes I would stay until dark, putting them on the top of the monuments so I could see the lights from my bedroom window. Once, I was so busy doing this that I lost track of time. It was late, and the gate was closed, so I had to climb over the fence to get out.

I was quite young at the time, but my mother wasn't the least bit worried. That's how safe it was back then. The only suspense in our lives came from my brother, Mitchell. He was always an adventurous daredevil. As soon as he could run, he played "squirrel," climbing trees and jumping from branch to branch. Once, he fell and chipped his tooth; he was lucky he had not broken more bones.

I was just the opposite. I was a very cautious young child who did not like to get dirty. My mother often teased me that I could wear a white dress for a full week without getting a spot of dirt on it. She would chuckle when she recalled how I would run to her crying whenever I got my hands dirty. I was so dainty, I wanted her to wash them for me. Once after lighting candles for All Saints Day, I spilled some of the candle wax on my new, beautiful blue overcoat that Aunt Helena had made for me. When I came home, I was afraid to show it to my mother, so I tried to wash it myself. That only made it worse. Ultimately, my "aunt" reversed the material, and you could not even tell it had been stained. I still prefer neatness and simplicity.

When I was seven or eight years old, I felt more mature than children my age. I remember my mother telling me to go out and play with the other children. So I went out and looked at them running back and forth, chasing a ball. It looked so silly to me that I returned home. My mother was so surprised, she wasn't sure what was going on.

She just looked at me and said, "So you are back already?"

I replied, "I'd rather read."

I liked to read biographies of famous people or fairy tales. I still remember the stories. Some of my memories go back even further. From a very early age, not quite two years old, my mother taught me to take care of my brother. Once, I remember when my parents were building our house, my mother was very busy. My brother, Mitchell, started to cry, so she told me to dance and sing for him. I have no idea how I sounded or looked, but whatever I did stopped him from crying. Later, as he grew, it was much harder to keep track of him. My mother continued to expect me to be responsible for him. But he would be climbing trees and swinging from the branches. I could not even climb a tree let alone keep up with him. My mother never knew what to expect from Mitchell; he would often come home with all sorts of unexplained scrapes, scratches, and even broken teeth. These memories might seem like minor incidents to some, but they remain meaningful to me because they take me back to a time when all was well with me and my family.

Lesson: Happiness doesn't come from achievement. Happiness comes from our souls.

At the age of six, like all children, I was excited about finally getting a chance to go to school.

Our school was located one kilometer from our house. We had wonderful neighbors. Some were Polish, but others were Russian and Ukrainian. Because of the diversity, my first day in school was very memorable as children of various ethnic and religious backgrounds gathered in the school yard. But, some of the children looked me over and thought that my golden blonde hair and brown eyes did not go together. My nails were so pink and shiny that they thought my mother had painted them. They made fun of me and criticized me from head to toe.

I felt relieved when I met the teacher. Each of us had to introduce ourselves. When it was my turn, I said my name: Regina Engelhardt. She greeted me, saying, "Do you know who you are?" I did not know what she meant. I repeated, "I am Regina Engelhardt."

(My family dates from the fifteenth century with roots in countries near the Baltic Sea like Germany, Poland, Lithuania, Latvia, and Switzerland as well as Canada. Only later in grammar school, as we studied Polish, Russian, Ukrainian, and German, did I learn that Taras Shefchenko, the Ukrainian poet, was born on the Von Engelhardt Estate near Odesa. Much later, as an artist and cosmetologist, I discovered that one of my patrons, Mrs. Brand, was born in Engelhart, a town in Canada. The town's founder had eliminated the letter d in his family name. My father's oldest brother, Adam, who came to the United States 150 years ago, and many other Engelhardts did the same thing. So the Engelharts and Engelhardts are often related. In the late 1980s there was a reunion of the Engelhardt family in Poland, but I did not attend due to other commitments.)

There was no other Regina in the class either. It was considered an unusual name, and that embarrassed me at first. I don't remember what I was saying to the other children, but it caught my teacher's attention. She turned around and said, "Philosopher, come here." I did not understand what she meant and thought to myself, *Is this my new name?*

When I returned home, I was so upset I cried and told my mother I refused to go back to school. "There is no other Regina. Why did you give me such a name? You could have named me Teresa or Maria or some other name like somebody important. Nobody wants a name like Regina."

My mother asked our priest for help. He came and calmed me down by explaining that my name was special and meant "queen." He assured me that I should be proud to be called Regina. (Through the years, I attended school in four different countries and never met another Regina. Now I can sign my artwork with my first name only: Regina.)

When I returned to school the next day, I met a beautiful girl named Teresa who had dark curly hair and blue eyes. We became best friends. From then on, I enjoyed my school immensely. My studies were fascinating, and I was thrilled when my teacher involved me in the theater. I recited poetry, danced, and sang, playing many different roles. Later, I joined the church choir.

My father's parents lived next to us. So every morning, before I went to school, I would go to my grandmother and ask her to tie a ribbon in my hair (poor Grandma). My mother was creative, but for some reason I did not think she knew how to do it. Besides, I liked visiting my grandma before hurrying off to school.

In our class, there were some very poor children including a Jewish girl who was always very hungry. I was a poor eater, so I would give her my lunch. I was so happy she finished it all so I didn't have to eat it. But on the way home, I would stop at my father's hair salon for men and women, and ask him for a few cents. Then, I would buy chocolates and munch on them as I skipped along the trail leading to our house. I was more than satisfied.

I enjoyed having so many friends from different nationalities and religions. We learned from one another, and everyone got along well. We even celebrated holidays together. There was a Greek Orthodox Church nearby, so my girlfriend and I would attend every wedding ceremony and watch how they held crowns over the heads of the bride and groom. The singing was outstanding. During Jewish holidays, I would go to the Orthodox Synagogue, and see how they prayed. I learned that women had to cover their heads, and sit in separate sections away from the men. In reformed synagogues, the women could sit together with men. During Christmas, my girlfriends would come to our house.

One day, on the way home from school, I was walking alone through the woods when three boys jumped out from the bushes and said, "Hey, you, Jew … We are going to kill you!" I looked around and realized they were talking to me. I had never heard any hateful comments against Jews before then. I was not Jewish, but I did not try to correct them. I did have Jewish friends, so I just turned to face them. I was scared, but stood my ground. I stamped my foot and said, "Come on!"

There was no one around, and they could have really hurt me. But they looked at me with big, frightened eyes and ran away. I was only eight years old, and no one had taught me to stand up to bullies like that, but it worked. They did not bother me again. I wonder, now, if they actually saw my Grandma Wardach's spirit behind me. She died when I was two years old, but she sometimes visited me as a child, appearing in my room unexpectedly and hovering close to my bed.

Now, I don't know for sure if she was with me the afternoon those bullies ran away, but I did learn a valuable lesson about not being afraid. I don't believe in running. I believe in facing problems and not letting them stand in your way.

Lesson: We must stand up to evil forces.

The first time I actually saw my maternal Grandma Wardach was on New Year's Eve, 1938. My parents had gone out and my dad's mother, Grandma Engelhardt, stayed with me and my younger brother, who went to bed earlier. Around eight o'clock, Grandma told me to go to bed. But, when I entered my room and pulled the cover from my bed, I noticed a strange woman standing in the bedroom doorway. She was tall and slender and stood still as she smiled at me. I did not know who she was, so I called out to my Grandma in the next room. The woman said nothing; She just continued to stand there and smile. I became more and more frantic and continued to call my grandma. I could not understand why she was not responding when she was just around the corner in the kitchen, praying the rosary.

Finally, I jumped into bed and ducked under the covers, peeking out occasionally to see if the woman was still there. I waited, fearful of what might happen next. After a while, when I looked and found the woman had left, I ran to the kitchen and told my grandma that I had been calling out to her because there had been a strange woman at my bedroom door. My Grandma Engelhardt did not believe me. She had not heard my screams. She just told me to go back to bed.

I obeyed her but did not sleep well. When my parents returned home the next morning, I told them my story. My mother asked me to describe the woman and what she wore. From my description, my mother recognized the visitor as her mother (my maternal Grandma). She had been buried in that dress. Nobody understood what the vision meant, but my Grandma began coming to me on and off after that

Then, in early September, 1939, around ten o'clock, my friends and I were playing in front of our house. It was a brisk, fall day, but the sun was shining, and the autumn leaves looked beautiful. Suddenly, we saw airplanes flying overhead, and we started to wave at them. At that moment, we noticed something black falling through the sky. We dropped to the ground, frightened, listening to explosions. One bomb had fallen behind our house and had exploded. None of the bombs that fell in our front yard, where the children had been playing, exploded. No children were harmed. But we realized we were at war.

Men from our neighborhood got together and disposed of the bombs without any incidents. Now I know that my maternal grandmother's spirit had protected us.

CHAPTER 2

THE INVASION

Lesson: The only enemy we have is ourselves.

When Russian soldiers entered Poland from the east and the Germans from the west, Poland was divided.

Our family and neighborhood were under Russian occupation. The stores and banks were closed because the soldiers were looting and stealing all they could. Thank God for our maternal Grandfather Wardach who was a big landowner. His property neighbored another large plot owned by another Engelhardt, not directly related to our family. Grandpa Wardach gave us a cow, pigs, chickens, bee hives, rabbits and grains. We were able to survive and even share with our neighbors. My parent's house had an extra lot where my mother grew vegetables and fruit.

Necessity truly is the mother of invention. During that time, people were creating beautiful things out of nothing. Everyone was resourceful, even my younger brother. He loved machines and would take things apart and rebuild them. To this day, he still tinkers with various mechanisms and creates new devices. Back then, though, we did it because it was a means of survival. At that time, everyone helped each other to live. Hard times had brought out the best in all of us.

Everybody was using their talents. My parents built special sheds for the chickens and rabbits. My mother planted a beautiful garden full of different vegetables and fruit trees, even red currants to make wine. We had a cow that gave us milk, so my mother made butter, cheese, buttermilk, sour cream and yogurt. She made her own soap too. For the winter, she made barrels of pickles, sauerkraut, fruit jams and raspberry juice (good for healing & preventing colds). We had plenty for our family and to share with our neighbors. I helped my mother stone-grind (hand-mill) the grains that Grandpa Wardach gave us. She made bread and shared the grains with others as well.

I remember when the stores were closed, and no one could buy anything. I needed boots for the winter. My mother made me some boots to match my winter coat, a cornflower blue coat. She put leather on the soles and trimmed the top of the boots with rabbit fur. When I wore these to school, I was fearful that the other children would laugh at me. Instead, they all admired my boots.

We had angora rabbits, so I helped spin the angora on the spinning wheel to make threads so my mother was able to knit sweaters and a beautiful hat for me for the winter. We also made wool threads, which meant my mother was able to knit gloves, socks and house-slippers. Her hands were always busy, knitting, crocheting or sewing. Since we lived during uncertain times, my mother was always preparing and packing food by drying the meat and bread to keep it from spoiling. We had to be ready to leave the house at any moment.

There were bullets, guns and dead bodies lying around. One time, my brother and his friends gathered some bullets and put them into a bonfire away from any other people. But my mother did not know where he was, and sent me to find him. As I approached, calling out his name, he screamed, "Regina, lay down on the ground!" As soon as I flattened myself onto the ground the bullets started flying over my head. I could have been killed.

Another time, my brother found a machine gun on our property and took it apart. My father challenged my brother to put the gun back together. My brother did just that. He went to Grandpa Engelhardt's tool shop and took what he needed. When Grandpa went to his shop and found his tools missing, he wondered who had taken them. Then it dawned on him to go to our house to see if my little brother was the one. Sure enough, that's where he found them. When my father came home from work he noticed that the gun had been reassembled. So, he tested it and was very impressed. It actually worked!

After our family moved to the United States, my brother worked in a tool-and-dye shop. When machines came from Japan and had to be assembled, people, who were engineers, struggled. They asked my brother to help. He assembled them without looking at the instructions. They asked him, "What engineering school did you go to?"

He said, "None." He had never even finished high school. He never liked doing the homework. From the time Mitchell was in grammar school, I either did his homework or helped him with it. A few minutes before we had to go to school, he would ask me, "What did you do here?" As I would explain it to him, he would nod and say, " okay." He used to get A's, B's and C's, but he never failed.

When my brother bought his first house, he finished the basement on his own. When his friends saw what he had done, they asked him to do it for them. Now he lives near Lake Huron, Michigan in a house tucked nearly a quarter of a mile from the road. He actually built a small light house on his front yard, near the road. People who see it are so amazed they often stop and ask who built this. When he tells them he made it, he gets lots of orders for more.

One day, his wife decided that she would like to have an extra cabinet for their dining room. He built one and matched it so well to their furniture that no one can tell that it is not part of the original set.

Lesson: We discover the talents we are born with in times of need. That is how the difficult times bring out the best in all of us.

During Russian occupation, the schools were open, so we were able to continue our education. But Russian schools were a year ahead of Poland's schools. I had to go back to the fourth grade where we used the books from the fifth grade. I did very well and earned a golden diploma with pictures of Lenin and Stalin on it. In Russian schools, to receive the golden diploma, students must earn A's on all the questions asked throughout the school year. There is a board on the wall with every student's name where the teacher marks their grades. At the end of the year, there are oral and written exams. Each student pulls a card with questions on it. The teachers sit at the table and judge. If all the answers are correct throughout the year and during the final exam, then the student earns the golden diploma. Another thing that was beneficial in Russian schools is that the first class everyday was gymnastics. The students would get energized by the physical exercise then they were ready to sit and concentrate on their studies.

However, there was a lot of tension under Russian occupation. My aunt, my mother's sister, Helen, was married to a rich landowner near Minsk. She and her family were all killed by Stalin's Russian forces, simply because they were "rich." Their land then became community property. Meanwhile, Russian soldiers were staying with us in our home as well as with our neighbors. They were young soldiers awaiting their call to fight on the front lines. They ate their meals with us, slept in rooms we provided them, and shared our outhouses. We had no running water or electricity. We all had to share well-water for all our cooking, hygiene and other needs. But they had to be ready to drop everything at a moment's notice to leave for the front.

A lot of people from east Poland were shipped to Siberia. Families in random neighborhoods were picked up and taken away in the middle of the night. The soldiers seemed to target bankers, teachers, businesspeople, professors and anyone of influence who could potentially rally support for a resistance movement. We were on the list to go, too, because my father owned his salon and knew lots of people in all walks of life, including in the government. It was, in fact, the Mayor who warned my father that we were listed. For eight months, we slept fully-clothed with boots and all because the trucks would always come to take people away in the middle of the night. As soon as the soldiers entered the house, no one was permitted to move; they had to file out to the trucks exactly the way they were. It was winter, and it was quite cold and snowy. So, lots of people died of exposure on the way to Siberia. The soldiers would just open the doors of the train cars and throw the bodies into the snow. Luckily, two weeks before the date of our evacuation, in 1941, Hitler declared war on Russia. Then we were under German occupation for two years. During that time, all schools were closed.

Private teaching was illegal, but my father's friend, who was a professor, came to "visit" us. He stayed and actually taught my brother and me. (After the war, when I went to high school, the teachers gave me a test, and decided that I belonged in the second year of high school).

As the war waged between Russia and Germany, the Ukrainians started a revolution. Ukrainian rebels started killing everyone who was not Ukrainian, even German soldiers. People had to hide underground in the wooded areas to avoid the soldiers and the Ukrainian rebels who were raping and murdering everyone in sight. The Ukraines used crude weapons – knives, hayforks, axes, and anything with a blade. Once we found a German soldier's body near our house. His ears were cut off, and a Swastika was carved into his chest.

A lot of Jewish and Polish people hid in the woods in larger underground shelters with covered entrances behind bushes. Many Polish people helped Jewish people by delivering and providing necessities of life to these hideout bunkers. Some Polish people hid Jews in their homes or farms as workers. Some helped them by smuggling them to Hungary, and from there, to Argentina or Israel by changing their names to Polish names.

We built our bunker as soon as war broke out in 1939. My parents picked a spot in our garden amid the tall sunflowers to dig a hole deep enough for the adults to stand up. It was very sparse, with dirt walls, floor and ceiling and only enough room for our family members to hide. The entrance was a small opening like a rabbit's hole, so we all had to crawl through to reach the bunker. There was no furniture or food in the bunker. The only light came in through the narrow entrance. If there was no bombing and there were no soldiers nearby, we would live in our house. We used our bunker to hide in whenever fighting came too close to our home — whenever we heard warplanes overhead or heard explosions from fallen bombs or the rattling exchange of machine-gunfire nearby. Sometimes, it was only for a few hours a week. Other times, as the frontlines of battle crossed our land, we would be forced to spend many hours in the cold darkness of our bunker, listening to the incessant sounds of war above and shivering waiting, straining for cues of safety. Quiet was a common signal for us to check if it was safe to dash home for some food or rest. We could not sleep standing up.

Once, my mother warned me not to leave our bunker. But I was very restless; it was so beautiful and sunny outside I could not resist. I did not hear any shooting, so I ventured out into the garden. Suddenly, I noticed a soldier walking near the fence and looking down at the ground as if searching for a bunker opening. Fortunately, he didn't gaze in my direction. I stood very still, amid the tall sunflowers and tried to blend in. If he had seen me, I would not be here today.

Other times, when soldiers were all around us, we could stay in our own home to sleep because even the Ukrainian rebels did not want to engage in direct battle. As Hitler was moving deeper into Russian territory, he mobilized some men from occupied countries. Some of our neighbors were even drafted by the Germans. Once, we had a group of young Hungarian soldiers staying with us and with our neighbors. They were waiting to be shipped to the front lines in Russia. In the meantime, many of the soldiers enjoyed getting together with the young people in the neighborhood to play music, dance and sing at our neighbor's house. One night, the soldier who stayed in our house, said, "Let them go. I will stay with you and teach you how to speak Hungarian." I still remember all the phrases he taught me:

Szepkis lany (**sip-**kishliny): pretty girl;
kicsi baba (kichi ba-**ba**) little baby girl;
Koszonom szepen (**Kes**-enem **Say**-pen) Thank you very much;
Jonapot (**Yo**-napot) Good day;
Joreggelt (**Yo-**reggel) Good morning;
Viszont latasra (**vi**-son-**la**-tashra) Good-bye;
Cica (**tsi**-tsa) cat;
Kutya (**ku**-tia) dog.

In autumn of 1942 when the weather was getting colder, and Germans were having a difficult time, Ukrainian bandits became even more aggressive. They were burning whole villages all around us and killing people in their homes during night raids in the outskirts where we lived. Our neighbor, who was Ukrainian and a good friend, warned my father that the Ukrainian bandits told him to kill our family, or they would kill him and his family. The bunker saved our lives many times. But it could not protect us from Ukrainian raiders. Every night before sundown, we would walk about one mile or so into town, where it was safer, so we could sleep in a friend's house. We never knew what to expect when we returned to our home in the morning. We were always relieved to find it untouched but we were still wary and would search under the beds and behind furniture to make certain that there was no one still lurking, waiting to attack us.

One cold morning, one of our neighbors found a two-year-old Jewish girl near the wooded area and brought her home. The child had frozen feet and was very hungry. My father's brother and his wife, who never had any children of their own, helped abandoned children. They wanted to take care of that little girl. When we went to meet her, she looked at my mother and ran to her, calling "Mama."

The Germans wanted to kill her because they thought she was Jewish. But my aunt told them that she was Polish. Because of the war and revolution, there were Polish people hiding in the woods as well. What really saved this little girl was how she failed to respond when the Gestapo spoke to her in German, which sounds similar to Jewish. She acted as if she had not understood. So the Gestapo allowed her to stay with my aunt. Every night when we had to leave our home for the safety of town, I carried this little girl in my arms all the way.

We lived right across the road from the cemetery. Every day, I would see wagons bringing dead people who had been mangled and murdered by the Ukrainian marauders. One day, I decided to go to the cemetery and see them up close. The people from our neighborhood were digging one big grave, and women were washing the bodies to put them into the same grave. I will never forget the sight of an eight-month-old baby whom they found crucified to the wall. They counted 25 knife wounds. My cousin, a beautiful girl, was also among the dead. Her eyes were wide open and her arms and legs were twisted and bent in unnatural angles. Another woman who had been pregnant was sliced right open from her sternum to her pubis with her womb exposed and empty where her unborn baby should have been.

I ran home and could not eat or cry. I believe I even stopped growing. I remained in shock, unable to weep, until I was at least twenty four years old.

Lesson: Life is just. It breaks everybody's heart.

During that same period, my mother's only and youngest brother, Julian, was killed on his property as he left the bunker. German soldiers shot him dead as he tried to open the doors of his burning stables to free the horses trapped inside. One of his sons had been drafted into the German army and was killed in battle while fighting in a tank. The younger son was taken to Germany, and his daughter, Stephanie, who was pregnant, was found impaled on a pole with her hair pulled out, murdered by Ukrainian bandits.

In February 1943, when the Germans were retreating, they took our whole family and many other people with them as forced labor.

Their country needed workers as their men were drafted for the war. A lot of soldiers were dying because of the deep snows, the freezing cold and lack of food on the Russian front. Nobody in those days could win a war with Russia in the winter. Napoleon and Hitler each tried and each failed.

We had only one hour to prepare to leave our home, never to come back. My parents knew that this would happen and were more-or-less prepared for it when the time came. My mother was drying meat, bread and fruit so we would not go hungry. They had luggage already packed with some dried foods, clothes and important documents like birth certificates, identification records, and family treasures like a wool wall-hanging she valued. But my mother was packaging necessities up to the very last minute. We even put our jewelry and coins into our pockets which came in handy later when we were in displaced persons' camps. We used the coins/jewelry to barter for food and other necessities. I grabbed my doll, which my mother had bought for me only two weeks earlier. I tucked her under one arm, tucked some books under my other arm and told my mother I was "ready." My mother looked me over and quipped, "That's what you are going to eat?"

I looked at her and thought to myself, *I have my mother; she takes care of that.* That's how children think. Indeed, my parents carried the heavy luggage. Everyone could take whatever they could carry. But some people tried to take too much and ended up dropping the luggage and walking away.

The Germans were taking us to the Ghetto in Bialystok. After only one hour on the cramped train to Bialystok, the train hit a mine. Luckily, the soldiers who had inspected the railroad had found one mine and disabled it. The other two had been placed parallel to each other, so when they exploded the train popped up then came right back down onto the track without rolling down the hill. A little girl standing next to me started to cry. Without thought or hesitation, I handed her my favorite and now only doll. She stopped crying immediately. We had to leave the train and wait for a long time in the deep snow for another train to pick us up. I never saw that little girl or my doll again. Because of the long hours of waiting in the snow for the next train, my toes froze. I nearly lost one to frostbite.

However, God never forgets what we have done for others. Many years later, He gave me three daughters. I used to call them dolls. At that time, I did not know why. Now I do. Then when I became a cosmetologist, I used to tell my customers, "I feel like I am playing with dolls again," not realizing why I felt that way. Years later, I began to recognize the connection. Now I have three granddaughters and two grandsons.

> *Lesson: The only things you take with you are those you give away. The good deeds will become memories that pass on from generation to generation. At the same time, they will go with you as your diploma for a job well done.*

The little Jewish girl, whom we called Wladyslawa (after my uncle), was unofficially adopted by my aunt and uncle. She stayed behind in Poland with them. The man who had found her knew her parents and where they were hiding. He kept in contact with them as well as with my father's brother and his wife. After the war, we found out that Wladyslawa had been reunited with her parents and moved to Israel. My aunt and uncle had also been forced to leave their home and property for Szczecin in northern Poland near the Baltic Sea.

When we arrived at the Ghetto in Bialystok, we had to take a shower, first all the women and then the men. When I came out of the shower, I put on my old clothes but my shoes and socks were gone. The Gestapo told the people that no one would be allowed to leave the room until my shoes were found. After a short time, the shoes appeared but not my socks. I had to trudge through deep snow to the barracks without socks. My mother was worried that I would get sick. Everyone was labeled with a letter P. My family was skipped because we had such a well-known and respected German name, Engelhardt. My mother had boldly criticized Hitler and refused to be treated /labeled as German even though her paternal grandmother was also German. My mother said she was embarrassed

18

to be of German heritage because of what Hitler was doing. My father worried that the soldiers would retaliate and kill us because of my mother's stubbornness. Still the Gestapo did not harm us, but they refused to label us with the white letter "P" for "Polish."

We stayed in camps of wooden barracks with as many as 150 people in one room. We slept on straw mats on the floor and on bunked platforms – all packed together like sardines. There was one bathroom for all to share. It had just one toilet. We had no regular baths or showers except for the communal showers which were determined by the guards. There was very little food, and even the soldiers guarding us were hungry. They fed us only once daily; everyone would line up outside to get one bowl of thin soup. Sometimes we also got a piece of bread. Early on, we supplemented with whatever foods we had packed and carried with us – portions of dried meats and breads. We were trapped like prisoners and could do very little all day. There was no space to move. Only lots of time to wonder what would become of us.

My father had brought some money with us, so my family took a chance and sent me, a child, to the Gestapo office to seek permission to leave the compound to buy bread from a town bakery nearby. The officer in charge seemed to like me, maybe because I reminded him of his children. He let me go but told me I better come back. There was no place to escape. It was winter and we were at war. I was young and obedient, and I would not leave my family. Because I came back, he let me go "shopping" for bread whenever I asked. We tried not to ask too often, but each time I did, the same officer allowed me to go. After my first successful trip, other families also asked me to shop for them. Each time I requested permission, the same officer would allow me to leave. He took a chance letting me go, but I earned his trust.

After eight months, as Hitler was retreating we were moved to Count Lenski's Estate in Lwuwek. The grand house was completely stripped bare of all its furnishings and his lavish possessions. Everybody was crowded into the barren rooms and slept on the floor. There was no room for me to lie down, so I leaned up against some suitcases and woke up the next day with terrible pain in my ribs where the suitcase had been wedged between them.

There, too, food was very scarce. I don't remember eating much of anything. It was there that I watched an infant take his last breath. The mother had tried to breastfeed but had no breast milk, and eventually the baby starved. He was too weak to cry, so he lay in her arms, looking peaceful to the end. While there, we also had more freedom of movement because the soldiers were pre-occupied and less strict with the children. I remember going with some other children to a store nearby and sharing some root beer. It was lusciously sweet and we enjoyed every drop.

After two months or so, we were moved again to Pabianice near Ludz. This time we were put into apartment houses with furniture. It appeared that the owners had been forced to leave in a hurry with only some small personal possessions — just like we had been forced to leave our house. Here, we felt like home. There was a table with chairs, so we could eat like human beings again. The food was still the same, whatever they gave us. But my mother unpacked some of our possessions to make it feel more like our home.

Our apartment was on the second floor. I recall discovering the power of the mind through the eyes. I played a game in which I would stare at the back of someone's head and will them to turn around to look at me. I stood on our balcony and focused my gaze on one of several Gestapo officers crossing the road in front of our apartment. I told my mother to watch because I knew that officer would turn around to glance at me. The officer I had focused on did, in fact, stop in mid-traffic to turn around and look up at us. My mother became frantic and pulled me into our apartment. She was afraid he would shoot us. He did not.

We were in Pabianice only several weeks before England became involved in the war and started to bomb Germany from behind the front lines. Shortly after that, we were taken to Berlin. We arrived one hour after some severe bombing. The smoke was still coming from tall buildings with one sign on the top still intact, identifying "Engelhardt Pharmacy." We could not go through the city.

The next day, we arrived at Hamburg where we were lined up at the train station in front of waiting buyers. First, a man bought our whole family. Then a woman, his cousin, Mrs. Lühn, came. She looked at me and told her cousin, "You have enough slaves, I like her. I want her."

He looked at me and agreed, "Eh, she is too young anyway. Take her." So she gave him twenty marks and took me. She and her family were very good to me. She was a war widow who lived with her son, Hans Jürgen, maybe two years older than me. She had a big estate, so she bought a few workers to help her. When I arrived at her house, a lady who worked in her kitchen looked at my hands and said, "You have beautiful hands, but they will change soon." I did not know what she meant. I thought to myself, *Why would they change?*

I was put to work in the fields, milking the cows, washing large milk cans and filling them up with fresh milk ready for shipping. Sometimes, I would help in the kitchen after dinner. We had to get up at four to be ready to work by five that morning. I remember sometimes I had to haul some supplies in a wheelbarrow. Once, I put too much in the wheelbarrow and it was too heavy for me. As I was trying to push it, it flipped over. I was so tired and frustrated that I cried as I reloaded everything and tried again. Finally, I just had to take some things off to move it and make several trips.

I awoke one morning and could not bend my fingers. They were so swollen; I was not even able to dress myself. I started to cry. The owner, Mrs. Lühn, came in and dressed me, then took me to the doctor. After his examination, he told her that my heart was enlarged. I had been working above my physical strength. From then on, I was assigned to milking the cows and other lighter work. The owner noticed that her son, Hans, liked me. Hans used to come to me as I was working and offer to help me. Sometimes, I let him help with the heavier duties, but most of the time I did my own work. Sometimes, he brought his accordion and played it for me. His mother was very happy about this and she moved me into her living area. She asked me to call her sister Tante (German for Aunt)

Herta and her mother, Uma (Grandma, in German). I celebrated the holidays with her family and even received gifts.

> *Lesson: Life likes to surprise us. Changes come when we least expect them. The secret is to do our best and leave room for God.*

The family was aware that Hitler was losing the war. People realized that the slaves would be leaving the country when Hitler surrendered. I did not understand why, but I noticed changes in the way we were treated. About that time, Hans Jürgen realized I would likely be leaving and he became physically ill. His mother asked me to stay at his bedside to make him feel better. I did not comprehend how sitting there would help him, but somehow it did. He was a very kind young man and so was his whole family. They treated me like part of their family. Tante Herta made a dress for me. And she and Uma taught me to crochet. I crocheted some doilies which I saved and treasure to this day.

As the allies closed in, there was bombing every evening, so we all had to retreat to underground bunkers often for the entire night. The farm had two or three bunkers in all that were much bigger than the one my family had built. They still were made of dirt walls, floors and ceilings. But more people could fit. The family made sure that they could accommodate the workers as well. There was still no room to sit or sleep. All of us were very tired of living underground night after night. One time, after three full consecutive days and nights of no sleep in the cramped bunker, listening to the noises of war above us, I said, "I'm going to bed" (in the bedroom they had let me use in their house). "Whatever will be, will be." That night, the British forces were bombing Hamburg. The alarms were going off, and we heard multiple explosions. I could see the city burning from my bedroom window.

After that night, Hitler surrendered.

CHAPTER 3

MY FAMILY REUNITES

Lesson: Love is free; Hate is costly.

In May 1945, people were released from the concentration and forced labor camps to go to post-war displaced persons' camps. Mrs. Lühn begged me to stay with her family, but I decided to go with my parents to the camp. I knew that my parents and my brother, Mitchell, had been working for Mrs. Lühn's cousin. So we found each other and moved to the DP camp. Our first camp was in Fallingpostel, just six kilometers from Apensen where I had been working for Mrs. Lühn.

Naturally, after the war, there was again a shortage of food. Every day, once a day, we stood in line to get a ladle-full of a cornmeal "soup." In the beginning, I went twice to Mrs. Lühn to ask for food. She was very good and generous to me even though her son, Hans Jürgen, was very upset that I had left. People were hungry, but we were so happy to be free.

Our first school after the war was in our first camp in Fallingpostel where we lived under British occupation. Our family of four crowded into one room inside of the military barracks. There was one kitchen, which we shared with the rest of the families in our barrack. The housing and one meal a day was provided by the government. In time, people became organized and many, including my father, began helping in different capacities. A few days after we arrived in Fallingpostel, we were told that people from the United States had sent clothing for us, and everybody had an opportunity to choose two items — one to wear and one to wash. We were very grateful for that. To this day, when I travel I carry one to wear and one to wash.

In a short time, my father started to work in the international Pentagon with soldiers from all the different countries that had been forced to join the German armies. Sometimes, the soldiers sent some food for us, and in the summer my father would fish in the nearby river.

There were many Italian soldiers who were drafted into the German Army, and now were waiting to go back home. There were many talented people. We were dancing, attending concerts, and I got involved in the theater. It was a happy time in our lives. We had nothing, but we were happy. It is true, less is more.

> *Lesson: If you are not happy poor, you are not going to be happy rich. Happiness is a choice.*

One summer day, a friend of mine was playing piano in the game room. Windows were open, and an Italian officer and some soldiers stopped at the window to listen and observe. I was standing at the piano near my father. The officer came in to ask my father if he would allow me to go for a walk with him, so we could get to know each other. My father gave him his permission.

As we were walking we passed a park, so he suggested that we go in and sit down on the bench. While we were sitting and talking he kissed me on the cheek. That was the first time any man had ever kissed me. I was so frightened, I shot up and ran home. He called after me, "Regina, come back. I didn't mean anything." I did not return.

I guess I wasn't over the fear of men. During the war, my mother taught me to hide from all men. The officer continued to drop by and talk to my parents, asking them to talk to me. He wanted to marry me and take the whole family to Italy. But at sixteen years old I was not ready. I wanted to go to school. But he kept visiting, taking me and my mother to concerts. I could tell he was a high-ranking officer because whenever he walked into the concert halls all the Italian soldiers would rise. But I never even knew his name.

The time for all the Italian soldiers who were drafted into the German Army was running short. They had to go back to Italy. They gave a good-bye dance party. I came to that dance, but I was dancing with another soldier when the officer arrived. When he saw me dancing with someone else he left without even saying good-bye.

At that time, there were many wonderful men who wanted to marry me. But I was not interested. I wanted to go to school. The schools were organized by the professors who were released from the camps after the war and were waiting to relocate to other countries. Just like the rest of the adults, they were paid by the government. Books and supplies were very limited. But we studied everything, Latin, English, French, Polish, science, mathematics and anything the professors could teach.

The students did not pay for the school, but we all pitched in to help the school run. We were assigned to peel potatoes for our school dinners. We ate the same meal everyday — potatoes and gravy for dinner. For breakfast, we were served oatmeal with unrefined oats (ofczanka) which we nicknamed "Plujka" (spit-meal) because we had to spit out the rough shells of the grains.

I typed articles for the school paper and was very active in the school theatre, playing parts in every show —from dramatic to comedic and musical roles. The shows raised money for the school, but the student performers were not paid. There were a few schools like that in different towns. But over the next few years, as people were immigrating to different countries, the student population was shrinking, and everyone who was left was expected to report to Rehden.

My brother, Mitchell, and I went to Rehden, near Bremen to continue our education. I lived in the girls' dormitory, and my brother stayed in the boys' dorm. We had very strict rules. There was still a shortage of food, so every morning we still ate "plujka" oatmeal and for dinner, potatoes with thin gravy. Later, if we were still hungry, we bought bread and put sugar on it. That was our dessert. We didn't have much, but we were happy. I remember entertaining the girls by doing gymnastics like a circus acrobat. I was so flexible I could bend backward and pick up matches off the floor with my teeth then poke my head through my legs.

It was something that I did with ease and took for granted. At the time, I didn't understand that it was a rare and valuable skill. For me, it was just a way to pass time and delight my friends before we turned in at night. We had to be in bed by eleven o'clock. But before we fell asleep, some students would ask me to wake them up at three the following morning, so they could finish their homework. And I did. That was another odd skill of mine. I could decide on a time and wake up at that precise hour without using an alarm. It was a necessity back then since we didn't have alarm clocks. However, to this day, I don't use any alarm clocks. I just think about what time I have to wake up, and I wake up on my own — at least fifteen minutes before that time.

Again, I joined the theater and secured roles in every play — dramas, musicals, comedies. My last performance was as Rosyna in "The Barber of Seville," and we had the opportunity to wear fabulous costumes from the Bremen Opera House. It was our graduation performance, and it was grand. Afterward, there was a graduation dinner. The Catholic Monsignor, who was one of the guests, asked the professors if I could sit next to him at dinner because he wanted to have a conversation with me.

As we spoke, he asked to which country I would be immigrating. When I told him Detroit in the United States, he replied, "Wrong town. You belong in Hollywood." He was very impressed with my performance.

After graduation, I was getting ready to join my parents. While I was attending school, they had been moved several times to various displaced persons' camps. My brother and I would visit them every summer between school terms until my brother quit school after his second year of high school. He was bored in school and did not like to do homework. Yet, he passed his tests with minimal effort. Still, he did not want to stay in school and chose instead to join our parents, and work in the camps. There, he performed various office chores and delivered mail.

In August of 1949, we were finally transferred to Bremenhafen, the port city from which displaced persons were sent to their approved destinations in the United States. We had waited five years for this opportunity. We had secured sponsorship from my father's brother, Adam Engelhardt. He had to guarantee that there were jobs for us as well as a place to live. While in Bremenhafen, we were examined by doctors to make sure everyone was healthy. I found out, to my surprise, that I tested positive for tuberculosis. I had no symptoms, but anything was possible living in such close quarters in the camps. The doctor was not allowed to let me proceed to the United States, but my mother implored him to take another test. This one involved swallowing a tube for gastric sampling that showed I was not actively sick with TB. I was thus permitted to travel out of the country.

We were placed on the General McRay, a very large transport ship that took us to New York. We were allowed to take luggage and personal belongings but, by then, we had only one small piece of luggage for clothes for the four of us. My mother managed to keep a few other pieces of luggage for our important documents and my school books. But we were not allowed to take any gold, jewelry or money except for two dollars and fifty cents per person. The Germans had confiscated all of our assets. We had to strip down to our underwear before boarding the ship to ensure that we were not smuggling any valuables. Some women had planned ahead; They popped jewels out of their necklaces and rings to stow in special hidden pockets they had sewn into the crotch of their underwear.

The hidden jewels helped them eventually get settled in the United States

After I had boarded and settled in, the captain of the ship asked me to work in his office to do some typing. Sometimes, I helped in the library as well. I did not get paid, but we were transported free of charge, so I was happy to work for my passage. The captain was very good to me, and the trip was quite pleasant. However, one day there was a major storm, and many people got seasick and began throwing up. Only as we approached land and began to notice a towering, stone figure brandishing a huge torch, did people become ecstatic. Some of them started cheering at the mere sight of the enormous structure.

It was the Statue of Liberty.

CHAPTER 4

A New World, A New Life

Lesson: Change is the only thing that is here to stay. There is no guarantee in life or anything on earth. But we have to remember that if life closes one door, it opens another to a greater opportunity.

As we landed in New York, the reporters surrounded me, maybe because I was young, and they felt that I would tell them the truth. They asked me if I was impressed seeing the skyscrapers and the cars. I said, "No, it is so dirty." Coming from Europe, where the people are trained from an early age not to put trash on the sidewalk, it was shocking to me to see bits of trash and papers flying in the wind, some blowing right into us and our faces.

Later, I was in line to buy lunch for my family, and several people approached to ask if I was Sonia Heni, the actress. I said, "No." They told me that she had visited New York the week before and had worn a hat like mine. Later, a businessman who was eating lunch at that train station came to me and asked if I would like to have lunch with him. He said he wanted to chat with me to find out more about Germany. He was of German descent. I agreed, so he saved me two dollars. I was relieved because the Germans had only allowed us to bring ten dollars for four of us to buy lunch in New York.

When we first arrived in Detroit, Michigan, from Europe in early September 1949, we were greeted by my father's oldest brother, Adam Engelhardt, who had left Poland at the age of twenty one. He had traveled to many states and finally settled in Hamtramck, Michigan. He liked the climate and the work opportunities there. We lived in his house for only two weeks before we were able to move out on our own. My Uncle Adam, his wife, Victoria and their children were very kind, generous and helpful. We stayed close even after my father and I found jobs that allowed us to rent an apartment on Lehman in Hamtramck and furnish it with used furniture.

The living room furniture was a "Christmas gift" from the architect, Bill Sanders, whom I met during the first week at my Uncle's house. My father met his father, and he brought his family to meet us. We became very good friends. Now I see that he was more than a friend — he was my special angel. He truly loved me. He was so attuned to me that I just had to think about something, and in no time, the telephone would ring. It was Bill checking to see if I needed help. He wanted to marry me, but I still was not ready. I wanted to help my parents get established in the new country, and I wanted to get acquainted with the new world myself. Bill was the most helpful and most generous man I had ever met. Eventually, Bill married somebody else. We remained very good friends until death did us part ten years later.

Bill was the one who discovered the artistic talent in me. I was doing architectural drawings for him, and sometimes I sketched on the side. One time, he came and looked at some of the drawings and asked me, "Who did this?" I told him I had drawn them. "Very good," he said, "I will see you soon." A while later, he returned with some paper and charcoal and told me to draw a portrait of a woman. He left, saying, "I will see you in half an hour." After a while, he came back with a drawing of the same face. He looked at mine and said, "Yours is prettier than mine." It was so natural for me to depict beauty that I often did not realize I was doing it until other people remarked on this tendency.

Three years later, when I was visiting Caroline Edmundson in her studio in Las Vegas, she was painting a portrait of a lady. I took pencil and paper and started to draw her as well. After we were done, she said, "Regina, you drew her prettier than she is."

Thirty years later, when I was taking art lessons, fellow students said the same thing, but the teacher said, "Nobody complains if you make them look better than they are." I presume everybody sees things differently.

My first job was taking care of an eight-month-old boy, Jimmy Tripp. I was a live-in babysitter. My only free day was Sunday and my pay was twenty dollars a week. After a few months, I found a better-paying job working as an office assistant to an ophthalmologist in Hamtramck. After about a year, my maternal uncle in Chicago died. The doctor fired me because I went to the funeral even though he had not given me permission to miss work.

It did not take long for me to find another job working behind the meat counter at Kowalski Sausage Co, where I stayed for several years. I was a natural at weighing cuts of meat. Often, I would weigh slices of meats in the palm of one hand before checking the weight on a scale. I was almost always right.

I also started studying mechanical drawing at Lasky Institute of Technology. I was the only woman in the class, and the teacher was very impressed with my work. Mr. Lasky was planning to write a book, and he asked me if I would do the illustrations when he was ready. I was very pleased and told him I would be honored to illustrate his book.

Around that time, I also joined the International Institute, a club where I met people from different countries who had settled in Detroit. The club was located on Kirby Street across the street from the Detroit Institute of Art. It was very interesting. We learned from each other. I met people from all walks of life – from actors to doctors from all over the world, including Poland and Iran. Some of the actors from the Warsaw Theatre remembered me from my performances in Germany. They invited me to join the Variety Theater in Detroit where I played a part in every show – comedy, drama and musical. My mother, who attended the performances, told me that she often overheard the audience comment on how I "embraced" the audience with my eyes. She had noticed it as well. Some business people who saw my performances offered to pay my way to Hollywood. But, I refused. I had been in the United States only one year and still had a strong accent, so I thought that the American producers would not accept me. Besides, since the age of fourteen, I had not been able to cry. If I had to cry for a role, I had no tears. I had to pretend.

When I went to Dr. Sandweis, he examined me and said, "Regina, your body is in shock. That's how God preserved you." I was frozen like Lot's wife, in the Bible. I didn't thaw out until I was almost twenty four years old. I remember feeling so happy when I could finally cry and there were real tears. I just started to cry for no reason. My mother asked, "Why are you crying?"

All I could say was, "I just feel so happy."

Lesson: You were born to shine. Don't tarnish your soul.

In the meantime, I started another chapter in my life. Since I was sixteen, I'd had a lot of marriage proposals, but I always turned them down. It was right after the war. I had only recently been freed from slavery, and I wanted to study and enjoy my freedom. Besides, no one was certain where we would end up or in which country we would decide to settle. Eventually, some of the displaced people went to Poland, some to Australia, Brazil, the United States, Argentina, Belgium and some remained in Germany. We waited over five years in camps in Germany before we finally could come to the United States — even though we had relatives there, and they guaranteed jobs.

When we arrived, I wanted to be free to organize my life and help my parents. Another thing that scared me away from marriage was the divorce rate. I had heard divorces were prevalent in the

United States. I was raised during hard times when people flocked together. Life was uncertain, and people were helping one another to survive. I told my mother I was not going to get married but would adopt a child. I really wanted to buy things and care for someone else. I was buying for my parents, but it was not enough. I needed a child. My mother opened my eyes when she remarked, "If you are not married, they will not let you adopt a child."

My decision to marry was based on fear, which is a negative emotion. At that age, I didn't know that any decision made when a person is afraid, angry or tired, is likely to be wrong. I had a lot of men to choose from. Sometimes, that also can be more confusing. I decided to choose Gerard Twardon, a man who had originally studied to become a priest. He didn't take the last vow, so he was free to marry. I assumed he had a good moral foundation and, therefore, we would never divorce. I met him at a picnic at Orchard Lake near the seminary. When we first encountered each other, we were swimming in the lake. He swam close enough to me that he happened to brush up against my body, and his body started to shake. I asked him if he was cold. His answer was, "No." I didn't really pay much attention to him. In fact, I forgot all about him.

Many months later, my Uncle Adam called me and said, "I received a letter from Orchard Lake addressed to you." I was surprised. I said, "I don't know anyone in Orchard Lake." I didn't want to pick it up. When my uncle delivered it, I read it, but I could not visualize who it was from, so I didn't open it for a long time. My job kept me very busy, and the theatre consumed the rest of my time. Then one day, I thought maybe I should open it and see who it is.

Lesson: Follow your first mind.

When Gerard Twardon, the author of that letter, first walked into our home to become acquainted with me and my family, I remembered how we had met. But my father's reaction surprised me. As soon as he shook his hand, he came to me and said, "Pick any man but this one." I was stunned, because my father never said anything derogatory about anyone. At that time, I didn't think very seriously about Gerard anyway. This was his last year to study to be a priest.

In the spring, we were invited to his graduation. My mother, my boyfriend and I decided to go. It was Sunday, a beautiful sunny day. As we were approaching a group of graduates standing on the steps — I looked at Gerard and had a vision. I saw him dressed in a top hat with tails and in that moment, I exclaimed, "Oh! The devil!" At that same moment, the thought came to me to turn around and go home. My mother asked me what I'd said. I was too scared of what I'd seen so I said, "Oh, nothing … nothing."

Lesson: We must listen to our intuition and act immediately. By ignoring it, we will make mistakes.

God could not have been more helpful; God could not have made it any clearer to me that this man was – like in the Bible – a wolf in sheep's clothing.

After graduation, the professors were hesitant about ordaining Gerard. He was disappointed, but after some time, they decided to proceed with his ordination. But by then, he had changed his mind and refused to be ordained. In the meantime, I was busy with my life, dating, acting in the theatre, working and meeting new people.

One Sunday, Professor Domaracki, who was teaching at Montreal University, was visiting his friends in Detroit. By chance, he saw my picture in the newspaper advertising a musical in which I was starring. He immediately told his friends, "This is going to be my wife." His friends had my telephone number, so he called and asked if he could come over to meet me. I agreed.

When he arrived, since he was a nobleman from Poland, he acted like one. He introduced himself to my parents and me. Then he proceeded to tell my parents that he came with the intention to marry me. He told my father, "You know I cannot marry just anybody!" He said that he was the last of the Domaracki family, and his Grandmother had a Villa in Capri where we would go on our honeymoon … that I would need jewelry, of course … and so on and so on.

As I was listening, it scared me. I thought to myself, *What could I offer him?* We had only been in the United States two years and we had been allowed only to bring ten dollars for four of us to buy lunch in New York. By the time we met, I had already accrued some savings. But, I had been bought as a slave when I was fourteen years old, so what popped into my mind was that he was trying to buy me. I know he was doing everything right, but maybe because it was happening so fast it scared me. I understand him now. He lived far from Detroit and could not come to see me often. He did not have the luxury of taking time for us to get to know each other better. He knew what he wanted. He was older and mature, so he didn't want to waste any time. After he went back home, he began sending letters special delivery every other day. They were short notes, but the message was clear: He loved me very much, and he really wanted to marry me.

My parents, Maria Wardach and Marian Engelhardt, had had a similar experience. The third time they ever saw each other, they were at the altar, exchanging vows. Their marriage lasted until death, sixty four years. Through the years, I have learned about a lot of couples like that. One look across the room and that was it. Those glances resulted in good, lasting marriages. But, at that time, I did not see it that way. This led to another decision based on fear.

We must be very cautious what we say and think. Thoughts are very powerful and words even more so. But, I suppose my mistake was meant to be, so I could experience and learn a lot in this lifetime. God could not have been any clearer or more helpful. He had sent word via Father Podezwa, a priest from Orchard Lake Seminary, who was working on his Doctorate degree at the Montreal University and knew Professor Domaracki. Father Podezwa came to our house for dinner and begged me not to marry Gerard. He said, "Don't marry (Gerard) Twardon; He doesn't know anything. Marry Domaracki, he really loves you." These were his words.

Three weeks before my marriage to Gerard, I had another wake-up call. I had a very strong intuition to call off my wedding. We must obey the inner voice without hesitation. I wanted to cancel, but then came another fear. I was concerned about the disappointment that the cancellation would cause to so many people. I thought, maybe I could make it work.

A week before exchanging vows, there was another close-call. In the Catholic Church, people who intend to marry go to see the priest for a brief lecture. I went alone, so the priest asked me, "Where is your future husband?" I responded, "He told me that he already knows all that." The priest got tears in his eyes and did not say anything more about that. But his reaction provided another insight that I wouldn't learn until it was too late.

> *Lesson: If he is not with you now, he is not going to be with you later.*

The day of the wedding, as I was standing in the church, Bronislaw Wroblewski, who was a composer from the Warsaw Theatre and was connected with our Variety Theatre in Detroit, came over to me and said, "All this talent into the kitchen?" During the exchange of vows, the voice inside of me was screaming, *Say No! Say No!*

I didn't speak, so one of the three priests officiating shook my shoulder, saying, "Say Yes! Say Yes!"

When I said "Yes," I felt as if a big stone was falling on top of my heart. As we were leaving the altar, I looked at the people. They were all crying. I said to my husband, "This is my funeral, not my wedding."

CHAPTER 5

TRUTH AND DELIVERANCE

Lesson: We too often say Yes out of fear instead of No out of love.

The reception was at the Town and Country Club. Only thirty people were invited. We traveled to Miami, Florida, for our honeymoon. On the bus to Florida, we met another couple who were also going on their honeymoon. We stayed in the same hotel. We even spent some time together on the beach and at dinner. One morning, my husband told me that he had made plans to meet the other man for breakfast. I asked, "What about me?" He answered, "If you want, you can come along." I was shocked and disappointed.

That afternoon, as I sat on the beach alone because my husband had decided to do something else with the other bride's husband, a young man passing by spotted the wedding band on my finger. He stopped and asked, "So where is your husband? He is making a big mistake leaving you alone. " Then he walked on. This was yet another warning sign from God. It had been a week since we had married, but our marriage had yet to be consummated. Even I knew that something must be wrong.

I decided to leave Gerard and go home to have our marriage annulled. I approached my husband to give me the money and the ticket, because I had decided to go home. (I had given him my money and tickets to make him feel like a man in charge of our finances so that he could pay for dinners, etc.) At that point, he finally tried to formalize our marriage. But by then, I did not want anything to do with him anymore. To my shock, he forced himself on me. I felt so nauseous, I could not eat breakfast. The restaurant owner joked, "You must be pregnant." I couldn't believe it! And it was not true. (It was actually two years later that I became pregnant).

> *Lesson: If something is meant to happen it will happen no matter what.*

My mother had tried to protect me during the war when soldiers were raping women and children. But, no one could protect me from my own official husband. After that rape, I felt trapped. The marriage was consummated, so I was stuck. I had to make it work now.

When I told my fellow actors that I would quit acting because I wanted to concentrate on being a good wife and mother, they begged me not to quit. Their advice was correct. All of them were older and wiser. They had life experience. They knew that my husband's background did not prepare him to be a husband and a father. He had lived too long in an all man's world, first the Army then the seminary. Neither prepared him for marriage. I tried to be a good wife. I worked at Henry Ford Hospital as a receptionist. He kept losing his jobs, so I was helping all I could. But the marriage simply was one-sided. He did not cooperate as a team. Even when he was not working, he would not pitch in at home.

After six months, I again decided to divorce Gerard. I had a meeting with Father Jasinski who was my husband's sponsor while he had been in the seminary. Father Jasinski told me then, "If you would have married the first man off the street, you would have been better off than with this one … (Gerard) Twardon owes me $7,000, but I will let it go." Gerard had never told me about his debts.

I went to Las Vegas and let Nada Novakovich (whose father was a Yugoslavian ambassador to the United States) handle my divorce case. I had no children, no properties; It would have been very simple. I stayed in Las Vegas for nearly two months until the divorce was to be finalized. I worked in a casino as a "starter," throwing dice and rented a room from a woman who had seen many women in my shoes. She advised me never to go back to Gerard. She wanted to take me to Hollywood. Nada also had several contacts in Hollywood and kept urging me to meet them. She even offered to fly me out there for free.

But, two weeks before the trial my mother called me. Gerard had come to her and promised that he would correct himself. He was taking a chemistry course at the University of Detroit. He sent me flowers and apologies. My mother told me that there were no divorces in our family, and that my divorce would bring shame upon our family.

Being very obedient, I canceled the divorce and returned home. We rented an apartment in Detroit. I took a job at the American Savings Bank where I started as a teller then became an administrative assistant to the bank's manager. Gerard worked in quality control at Ford Motor Company. I bought him a new car, paid for in cash, while I rode the streetcar downtown to my job.

Two years later, Miriam was born. It was a difficult experience for me and my child. My obstetrician, Dr. Smyka, told me, "No more children because you will die!"

I have to share the mistakes I made, so others can learn from them. On the morning of July 15, my water broke as I was getting out of the bathtub. At first, I was shocked. I was not sure what to expect, but I asked the lady in the downstairs apartment, and she told me to expect a baby to be born soon.

At the time, I had no pain, so I went grocery-shopping. I wanted to cook a few days worth of meals for my husband to eat while I was in the hospital. As I was cooking, I started to feel pain and pressure, so I went to sit on the toilet and that felt better. Then I tried to finish my cooking and baking. By five that evening, the pain was so severe I asked my husband to take me to the hospital.

Once there, I was too weak to talk. Luckily, a doctor was passing by and noticed that I was in pain, but not screaming. He immediately started preparing me for delivery. Later, he told me that I had waited too long; I could have had the baby in the kitchen.

Lesson: We women have to learn to love ourselves first.

The delivery was very stressful. I was very weak after working all day. My daughter's head was too big. The doctors were deliberating whether they would need to perform a Caesarian section but decided against it because they felt there was a possibility I wouldn't survive the surgery. So they applied forceps to her skull and squeezed her head to pull her through, bruising her shoulder on the way out. I still remember the last push I gave; I howled as loud as a lioness and lost my voice. When my husband came to see me and brought me flowers, the doctor warned him that I could not speak. I was too exhausted. The process left me in tears and kept me from sitting for a week. The baby and I stayed in the hospital for a full week to recover.

When it was time to bring me and the baby, Miriam, home, we could not find my husband. I had to call my sister-in-law to come and bring us home. I was concerned that maybe he had an accident, so we called the police. They told us there had been no accidents. They said," He's probably in a bar someplace!"

I could not believe it. "No, that is impossible," I insisted. "This is our first child!"

Gerard was missing for more than twenty four hours. The next day he arrived home drunk. At that moment, I understood that the seminary had not prepared him to be a husband or a father. He felt that children were my responsibility. Before the baby was born, I had quit my job to be a mother. A year or so later, my husband lost his job in the auto factory, so we had to move to my parents' house. I started to teach him mechanical drawings. But he was not cooperating.

Soon after, I was pregnant with my second child. As soon as my husband started to work at Chrysler Corp. in the quality control department, we bought our own house. It was a four-bedroom house so I was able to rent two rooms upstairs. We had $2,000 and I borrowed $1,000 from my aunt and $800 from my parents for a down-payment.

There were a lot of layoffs and Gerard lost his job again. So I again encouraged him to take a mechanical drawing course in school. He did. As long as I was helping and doing the drawings, he was getting A's. One day, my mother visited saw me doing the drawing. She asked, "Who is going to work?"

I said, "He is."

She said, "Not if you are doing the homework for him." She made me realize the truth. I quit doing his work and he dropped the course.

Then he decided to study chemistry at the University of Detroit (U of D). Again, he was failing so, again, I started to do his homework. I wanted to help him to succeed but he wouldn't apply himself. He had enough education to teach at U of D, like his friend suggested. But his answer was, "I like the lower kind (of people)."

The country was in a recession but, eventually, Gerard landed a job at Ford Motor Company, again in quality control. Yet, there were layoffs and strikes as always. Again, he was laid-off. The money that I collected from renting the two bedrooms was helping me put food on the table. One time, he actually took the money and went to the bar. That left me without money to buy milk for the baby!

When it was time for me to go to the hospital to deliver my second child, I asked him if we had insurance coverage, even though he was laid-off. He assured me we did. But when I was ready to leave, I realized that I had no insurance. I had to borrow $100 from John Grabowski who was renting a room in my house. Luckily, he befriended me while we were both in the Fallingpostel camp in Germany. He was a kind, generous man who became Godfather to my second daughter, Elizabeth.

In October of 1958, I asked my three-year-old, Miriam, what she would like for Christmas. She brought me a magazine that had a picture of a baby in a playpen and said, "I want a baby like this one."

I told her that she had a little sister, Elizabeth. She said, "She is blonde. I want a baby that looks like me."

I ignored the request but a month later I went to the doctor, and he told me that I was pregnant again. Miriam got her wish, though her gift did not arrive in time for Christmas. When I came home from the doctor's office and told my husband that I was pregnant, he said, "Oh, now you have to put up with me, no matter what I do. Nobody will want you with three children." He took his pillow and marched upstairs to an empty bedroom.

I was shocked and felt abandoned. Then I realized that Dr. Smyka had been right. He knew my husband before I did. After our first baby was born, Dr. Smyka told me, "Regina, leave him. He is going to keep you pregnant and barefoot." I became very ill. I had such stomach pains I could not eat or drink. My doctor kept blaming my symptoms on the pregnancy.

Finally, I went to Dr. Haszczyc who was a surgeon from Poland and had practiced in Germany. He also had been held in the camps and experienced atrocities similar to the ones endured by my family. He looked into my eyes and said, "You have gallstones. Go to your doctor and tell him to take X-rays of your gall bladder." So I did. Three days later, my husband came home at three o'clock in the morning and found me doubled over on our bed in awful pain. I was actually having a near-death experience of going through a tunnel of light. He called the doctor and was advised to take me directly to the hospital. When my husband called him in the afternoon for the results of the X-rays, the doctor initially told him there was nothing wrong.

A few hours later, though, I was in such horrific pain that I begged for pain medication. My husband found a pharmacy that was open all night and bought some. The next morning, I urinated blood. At that point, we went directly to Dr. Haszczyc at Doctor's Hospital. I was put on intravenous antibiotics to cure the infection before he could operate to remove my gallbladder. After a week or longer, my veins collapsed. One evening, an intern attempted to find a vein and was using such thick needles that I felt as if I were being crucified. My nurse, an older woman, had been watching. After he left without success, she asked me if I had a headache because she had one. She said, "I am an old nurse, but I have never seen anything like that!" And the next morning the entire hospital was talking about the incident.

A few days later, I had the surgery. Dr. Haszczyc asked two other doctors to assist him. Dr. Gordon and Dr. Feel, an obstetrician, worked to save my life and my baby's. I was four and a half months pregnant. We did survive, but the danger was not over. One evening I had an out-of-body experience. I was standing at the head of my bed looking at my body, wondering if I was dead or alive. I was not breathing. My mother came after work to visit me and she thought I was dead and started screaming. The nurse came and started to shake me, saying: "Breathe ... Breathe!!! Or you will die!" I was still outside of my body and looking down at it, wondering to myself why the nurse was being so mean to me. *"I am so good; I'm not bothering anyone,"* I was thinking to myself. At that moment, my spirit returned to my body. I remained in the hospital for another four weeks.

When I came home, there was a lot to do to get our house in order before the birth of the new child. While I was in the hospital, my husband painted the ceilings in the living and dining rooms. When he went to work, I decided to finish painting these two rooms. At that time, I received a telephone call from Mr. Lasky (of the Lasky Institute of Technology) asking me to illustrate the book he had finally finished writing. The opportunities were coming to me without me even looking for them.

> *Lesson: Anything from God comes easily. If it is difficult,*
> *it comes from ego.*

I was overwhelmed with all I had to do, however. So, without thinking it over, I declined.

After I finished getting my house organized, my husband was laid off again. I decided that I would have to go to work. But I had too many strikes against me. I was pregnant with an unemployed husband and two small children at home. I was sorry then that I had declined the offer to do illustrations for Mr. Lasky. A few weeks later, I was with my mother in Hamtramck and we noticed a sign for the Hamtramck Beauty School. My mother suggested that I become a cosmetologist. At first, I didn't think so, but then I decided to try.

The first day, I impressed the teacher and the students by answering some questions correctly. It seemed like everything was clear and easy. As I continued my training, my instructor challenged me, "Regina, anybody can comb hair after it is set (ironed or curled). I want you to comb without setting." So I did and still do to this day.

I continued to study until a month before my due date. The teacher asked me to interrupt my studies until the baby was born. The stairs that led into the building were too steep. So I took a break.

On the first of August in 1959, my husband took me to the hospital at four o'clock in the morning and I was admitted immediately. I heard some woman screaming, so I asked the doctor to go and help her. His answer was, "No, we are not concerned about the ones who are screaming, but the ones who are not."

The next thing I remember was opening my eyes. I was in a little dark room with no one around. I thought, "Where am I?" I was actually in the morgue. In that split second, a doctor opened the door and, seeing my eyes open, jumped, shook me and said, "You are strong like a horse; I have to call your husband." Then he called the nurses and told them, "Wheel her to her room and massage her back."

I heard the commotion, but I did not open my eyes for another two days. Then I had to learn to walk again. (That was another miracle.) As soon as I could walk while holding onto the wall, I called my home, because I felt that something was wrong with my child. It was. But my Aunt Victoria, who was helping care for my children while I was in the hospital, did not want to worry me and told me all was well.

After a week, I went home with a beautiful, dark-haired baby with luminous eyes. I introduced her to my daughters and told them her name was Renee. My then four-year-old, Miriam, was ecstatic. As I was feeding the baby, she kneeled at my chair and kissed my feet, saying: "Thank you Mommy for the baby. She looks just like me." I was amazed. We didn't have TV, so she could not have been imitating this expression of deep gratitude. My two-year-old, Elizabeth, on the other hand, was devastated and jealous. She stood in the corner and cried. For the first few weeks, Elizabeth would awaken whenever the baby cried and demand to be fed first. I had to prepare two bottles of milk and feed Elizabeth first so she could feel secure in my love.

When my mother came to help me, we noticed that my oldest child, Miriam, the four-year-old, was limping. My mother checked her foot and I heard her calling Dr. Haszczyc — she was trying not to upset me. When I saw her foot, I almost fainted. The doctor came and was able to save her toe. Our neighbor's daughter had taken Miriam for a ride on the back seat of her bicycle and my child's foot had gotten caught in the spokes. (My intuition in the hospital was correct. A mother, regardless of where she is, always knows when her child is in danger).

As I regained my strength and organized my home life, I returned to Beauty School to finish my training. After a while, my teacher, who was part-owner of the school, approached me and asked me what I intended to do after I finished. I told her that I intended to work. She realized my situation and decided to help me. She was a famous stylist and colorist. Her salon was in Detroit, near the entertainment center. A lot of her patrons were Opera singers and other entertainers. She invited me to work with her in her beauty salon even before I graduated from the school. She gave me school credits for my work and paid me for my time. So I had the opportunity to do hair and nails for many performers. After a while, she gave me a written test and I scored 96%.

Then it was time to go to Lansing, the state capital, to get my license. It was a three-day test; written, oral and practical. I did very well and received my cosmetology license. When I came back from Lansing, my teacher arranged an interview with the owners of Oakley Beauty Salon and told them that she is sending a "Cracker Jack" to them. I did not know what that meant, but I did not care what name they called me as long as they called me.

Normally, we would work on commission only but, in my case, the owner offered me a salary of fifty a week and commission. The first week I took in more than my salary; over a $100. So, automatically I continued to work on salary and commission. In those days (1959), hairdos cost only two dollars and fifty cents. The shop was beautiful and my clientele was elegant and wealthy. My business kept growing.

After two years, a beauty shop across the street called me and offered me 60% commissions. I accepted the offer and moved. My clientele followed. A short time later, owners of a chain of beauty salons called me and offered me 70% commission. I tried to talk the owner, Howard Weiss, out of it because I thought it sounded like 100% after he paid for the rent, water, gas, electricity and supplies. But he insisted, "You want it or not?" He was so determined, I accepted his offer. I was very happy working for him. My clientele and income increased.

After awhile, my boss decided to sell some of the shops that were not doing as well. So, he asked me to move to the one he wanted to sell to make it appear successful. My clients followed me, and the salon thrived. So he sold it at a higher price. He wanted me to return to one of his salons, but I decided to transfer to a more expensive salon where the prices were higher though my commission dropped back to 60%. I used to work until seven thirty or eight o'clock, then catch a bus and come home around nine. There would be some women whom I had served while in Beauty School, waiting at my house for me to do their hair. I used to take my children to the basement with me, because my husband would often go to the bar and our nanny was also gone for the day. After everyone left, around one in the morning, I washed, cooked for the next day and cleaned the house. Many times, I just changed my uniform, fed the children and took a bus to work without even sleeping. Often, my breakfast was a banana that I took with me and ate on the way to the bus stop.

As time went on, I felt exhausted. I thought that I would drop dead at any moment. My mother noticed and decided to send me to Florida for a week to stay with my Aunt Victoria who was vacationing there. We shared a room in her friend's condominium and enjoyed the warm weather. The fresh air and sun made me feel stronger. I came back to work, started to save money and bought a used car, paid for in cash. That saved me some time. I decided to continue to live in a celibate marriage, so the children could have a father-figure.

Lesson: Experience adds wisdom and helps us to deal with life. So, be grateful for becoming a survivor and go on.

In the late '50s and '60s, there were more layoffs and Gerard lost his job again. My patrons suggested that I let my husband take care of our children since he was not working. I decided to try that, but my five-year-old told me that their father would leave them alone and go off some place even when they were crying. I decided to get our nanny back.

After that, he got a job at Ford Motor Company in quality control on the afternoon shift. He was supposed to be home at eleven o'clock but, as a rule, he would stagger in at three or four o'clock that night. Sometimes, he would come with another man, both drunk. One time, when we had his friend, a priest from England, visiting and staying in our house, his friend was very surprised to see that kind of behavior. But I put up with it.

One day, my husband stumbled into the house around eight o'clock in the morning when I was feeding the children before going to work. My daughter, Miriam, looked at him and said: "Daddy, why are you drunk?" That made me realize that I was not doing my children any favor by staying in that kind of a relationship. I decided that very day that I had to divorce him. After all, I had no husband and my children had no father.

A few days later, when he was at work, I took my bedroom set and the children's bedroom furniture and moved to my parents' house. Then I filed for divorce.

Regina's first husband, Gerard Twardon and
children, Miriam and Elizabeth, 1957

Regina's second husband, Richard Konefke

Christmas as a family, 1968

Regina's mother and father,
Maria and Marian Engelhardt

A scene from a performance of the Teatr
Rozmaitosci in Detroit (1952). The actors are
Regina Engelhardt and Jan Madurowicz. The play
is a popular Polish romantic comedy, "Ladies and
Officers." The photo is in the History Research
Center, University of Minnesota, Minneapolis.

White sculpture of "Eve" in clay by Regina Engelhardt

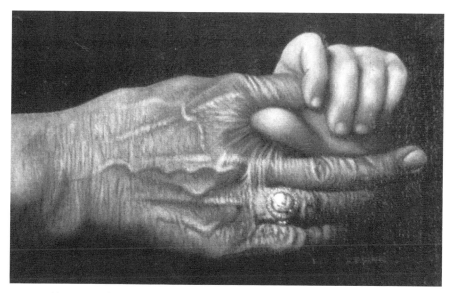

"Eternal Bond" oil painting on canvas by Regina Engelhardt. Prints are in seven countries, including the US.

Crowned eagle new symbol for newly-free Poland

By Robert Selwa
Staff Writer

Artist Regina Engelhardt is ready to place the crown back on the Polish white eagle, a sculpture she created for the American Polish Cultural Center. This sculpture will become the center's official symbol at its Crowned Eagle Ball today.

A newly independent Poland will be celebrated today by area Polish Americans.

Theresa Szymanski of Warren, chairman of the social committee of the American Polish Cultural Center, says the Crowned Eagle Ball to be held at 8 p.m. today at the center will celebrate Poland's new freedom.

The center, located at the northwest corner of 15 Mile Road and Dequindre in Troy on the Sterling Heights border, serves metropolitan Detroit's Polish Americans, with a membership strongly from Macomb County.

Highlight of the Crowned Eagle Ball will be the unveiling of a white clay sculpture of the crowned white eagle as the official symbol of newly independent Poland.

Szymanski said that since the 14th Century, the crowned white eagle has been the official symbol of Poland. When Poland lost its freedom to the Communists in World War II, the Communists who came to power changed the symbol to a white eagle without a crown. The crown was placed anew last year marking restoration of a lost heritage with the victory of the Solidarity trade and freedom movement as the new government of Poland.

Regina Engelhardt, a 61-year-old Detroit artist who immigrated from Poland, is the artist commis-sioned by the center to create its official symbol, the crowned white eagle standing atop a white clay model map of Poland.

Tickets for the Crowned Eagle Ball are $60 a person and available at the center, 689-3636.

Dancing to the Ted Sokolowski Orchestra will be in the exhibition hall of the center.

Newspaper article

56

Local artist's work exhibited

Regina Engelhardt, a painter and member of the Farmington Artists Club and Sculptors Guild of Michigan, has had one of her paintings depicting Princess Diana accepted for display as part of the permanent collection at the Althorp Museum in Northampton, England.

Engelhardt was inspired to paint the picture of Diana cradling an ill Pakistani child after Diana's death in a car crash last year.

Surrounding Diana in the painting are roses. Two on her right symbolize her children, one behind her symbolizes her former husband, Prince Charles, and a fourth rose on her wrist symbolizes her blossoming inner beauty. The background reflects her stormy life with a streak of light for the brief happiness she managed to experience just before her death.

Born in Poland, Engelhardt has lived in Detroit since 1950. Her original profession was mechanical and architectural drawings.

Since 1980, she has studied art with Sister Mary Ignatius at Mercy Center in Farmington Hills and has completed workshops at the Scarab Club in Detroit.

Engelhardt has had many one artist shows in a wide variety of categories and media – oil, pencil, watercolor, tempura and acrylic. In addition to painting portraits and sculpting busts, she likes to paint children, animals, birds, flowers and nature scenes.

She teaches art part-time at Mercy Center.

Portrait: *Local artist Regina Engelhardt's portrait of Diana is being exhibited in England.*

American Dream Festival
International
Art Challenge
presents this

Award of Excellence

to
Regina Engelhardt

on the 28th day of November, 1987

Congratulations on being selected as a finalist in this International Art Competition from over forty states and foreign countries. Your Work is a credit to the art community.

PRESIDENT

57

"Sharing Time" (clay) Regina Engelhardt

"Sisters," an award-winning pencil
drawing by Regina Engelhardt

"George," sculpture by Regina Engelhardt
depicts George Lukowski, a business owner,
humanitarian and collector of art.

"God of Peace" sculpture in white
clay by Regina Engelhardt

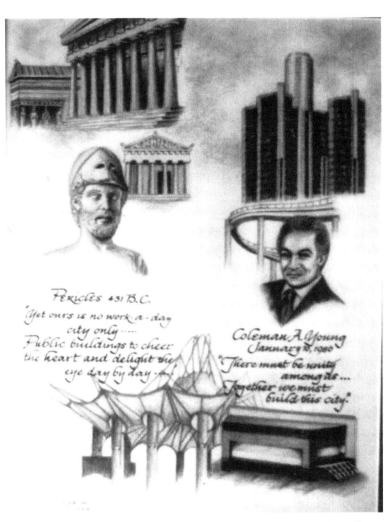

Within the drawing:

Pericles 431 B.C.
"Yet ours is no work-a-day
city only.....
Public buildings to cheer
the heart and delight the
eye day by day...."

Coleman A. Young
January 8, 1980
"There must be unity
among us ...
Together we must
build this city."

"Leaders" pencil drawing, a 1987 international
gold medal winner by Regina Engelhardt

"The Saint and Her World," Mother Teresa,
oil on canvas by Regina Engelhardt

"Best Friends," oil on canvas by Regina Engelhardt
won first prize in Michigan State Art Fair, 1988.

"Love and Harmony," by Regina Engelhardt, won the People's Choice Award in the International Art Challenge. Prints are in seven countries and twenty one states. A collector bought the original.

"Drummer Boy," life model in pastel,
Regina Engelhardt, 1981

Regina was named "The Flower of Poland"
at the Paderewski Foundation Ball.

Regina's family at granddaughter, Jacqueline
Gilchrist's and Clint Trigg's wedding.

Regina and her brother, Mitchell
Engelhardt and his wife Josephine.

"The New Dawn" by Regina Engelhardt (8-1-1997)

THE NEW DAWN

On August 1, 1997, I had a dream around seven thirty a.m. In the dream, a woman dressed in white with a touch of something blue, was floating in a bright, colorful sky. Her honey-colored hair was dappled with shocking pink Sweetheart roses. Her smile was subtle, like Mona Lisa's. I looked to my right and saw two buildings towering over other high rises and a cross atop a pale green church steeple with a smattering of trees.

I thought I was alone, but as I turned around I saw a woman with a table loaded with hair ornaments for sale. I asked her which one she would choose for me. She took one of them and pinned it to my hair. Not until I looked in a mirror on her table did I realize she had chosen a three-inch sculpture of the figure I had seen in the sky. I asked the woman, "Is this what you choose for me?"

She emphatically replied, "Yes" and abruptly turned her head away from me. That's the moment I awoke.

I knew this was a prophetic dream. Later that month, Princess Diana and Mother Teresa died a week apart.

Though I instantly named my dream "The New Dawn," it took me years to interpret it and discover why this mysterious figure was smiling. I decided to depict the dream with real and symbolic people who make positive contributions to our world. I painted people of different colors and creeds, living, loving and respecting one another. They must be the reason she smiles. The New Dawn is beginning to emerge.

CHAPTER 6

STARTING OVER

Lesson: Life's lessons are expensive, but they enrich our lives with kindness, compassion and gratitude.

My husband was giving me a hard time even after the divorce. I did not receive alimony. He only occasionally paid child support of seventeen dollars a week. When I took him to court, the judge told him, "So, pay her a dollar a week …" (to honor his agreement and show an effort to comply with his allotted responsibility toward supporting the children). That's when I realized that there is no true justice. I had to rely on myself only. Thank God, I was working. I had a good following but worked long hours. I managed to support myself and my children and even help my parents. Since my mother stayed with the children instead of working, I paid her for taking care of my children. My patrons were also always very generous to me. They brought me lunches and dinners, so I was even able to share with the clients who were hungry because they were coming for hairdos right after leaving work. I swear, the food seemed to multiply.

For many years after the divorce, my ex-husband wasted time and money, instead of developing a relationship with his children. He would hire private investigators to follow me and the men I was dating. One Sunday, after I came home from church, I noticed that he was driving around the house for a long time. It made me so upset that I started to itch. I went to the bathroom and took off my clothes and started to scratch myself. When I looked in the mirror and saw blood, I stamped my foot and said, "No man will ever do this to me again!" In that split second, the itch and bleeding stopped. To this day, it has never recurred.

> *Lesson: We have to take a firm stand and passionately declare what we want and don't want in our lives.*

When I took my husband to court, even the judge was surprised at his antics, saying, "You mean that eight years after the divorce, you are still chasing her?" For many years, even after I remarried, he kept calling me, threatening to kill our oldest child, Miriam. Sometimes, he and another man – probably his drinking partner – were on the telephone together. My second husband wanted to adopt my children, but their father would not agree to it.

As time went on and his health was declining, the woman with whom he lived wrote him a letter (which the children found after he died) letting him know that she "cannot take it anymore … (He) had to go!" He lived on his own for some time. As his health deteriorated, apparently he realized that he needed his family. I am sure that he was sorry for neglecting his children. He had not kept in much contact with the children before or after my second marriage.

Before I remarried, he would often not show up on Saturdays when he had visitation rights. My children initially looked forward to spending time with their father. They waited at the window for hours, watching for his car to appear, convinced he was just around the corner. Sometimes after waiting awhile, they called him to find out when he was coming only to learn he had no plans of seeing them that day. He would make up some excuse about his car. The last time he came to pick them up, he took my album filled with poems and other memorabilia from friends I had met at the school I attended in Germany. He also took a treasured letter from a famous, Polish Opera singer who lived in Canada. I had befriended the singer while on vacation with my aunt in Florida. Gerard even stole a special, three-foot-tall Miss America Doll that one of my patrons had given to my daughters. The doll was very expensive, so I had kept it in my bedroom as a collector's item. One of my clients had given me many other expensive toys and dolls for my children that had belonged to her daughter. When he brought the children home, he never returned any of the items, nor did he come back to visit the children. How sad; Instead of bringing them gifts, he stole from them.

After I remarried, he stopped using his visitations altogether and only rarely called to speak to the children. In most of those instances, he was drunk. By then, my children felt closer to my new husband, Richard, than to their father who had become a stranger to them. They did not know Gerard anymore and did not make it easy for him to get to know them on the phone. Renee, my youngest, would refuse to even speak to him.

One day, Gerard decided to surprise Miriam, our oldest daughter, who was living in an apartment above her landlady with a roommate. He came to her apartment while both Miriam and her roommate were still at work, but the landlady let him in to wait for her. He had pleaded and explained that he was Miriam's father, so she obliged. He was waiting in Miriam's room, in the dark when she walked in. He grabbed her and started to kiss her like a boyfriend or a husband would. Terrified, she screamed and pushed him away. She thought she was being assaulted by a stranger. After all, he had not seen the children in nearly fifteen years. Even when she learned who he was, she remained frightened of him. My new husband, Richard, asked a lawyer, who was his friend, to draft a letter to Gerard to let him know how Miriam felt and advise him never to contact her again. Shortly after that, Gerard died.

I remember when my daughter, Miriam, told us her story I had a feeling in my heart to try to persuade my children to go to him. I felt he was very sick and had finally begun to feel sorry for his behavior. Obviously, he missed his children and needed their acceptance. If he had been able to obtain their forgiveness, his death would have been easier. But, I did not enforce it because, at that point in time, it was too overwhelming for my three young, impressionable daughters.

Unfortunately, Gerard had never been a very healthy person. He had become infected with malaria when he was in the Army and was wounded during the war, leaving him with some kidney problems. His excessive alcohol consumption also contributed to his health issues. In fact, that's what killed him. He died of hypothermia in his own apartment after drinking too much alcohol.

As I look back, I am very grateful for my "Angels," who helped me to live a better life, showering me and my children with gifts. They are with me all the time. Even now, when I look around my house, I can still remember who gave me what. When I reflect on my life, I am more and more grateful for every experience, every person and every contribution those individuals made. I know that they enriched my life. Even my mistakes, were not really mistakes, but lessons. Each one ended on a positive note. God turns negatives into positives. Like a good parent, when we fall, He picks us up — if we cooperate by surrendering our will. Everything that God created has its purpose and it is good.

When the ego steps in, it throws us off balance. My belief is that before we are born, we choose the course and experiences to help us achieve what we want in this lifetime. God provides us with talents (the tools) to achieve what we want to achieve. God opens the door by giving us free will to change. That is why psychic people can predict the future so many years ahead of time. God gives us the opportunities, but it is up to us to accept them. I speak from my own experience. I believe that everything God creates is perfect. But as we go through life, the circumstances in which we find ourselves create very complex situations, forcing us to make choices that we are not always prepared to make. Often, we are like blind people groping for the right road, the right turn or right place. Sometimes, we make a good decision, and sometimes we make the wrong move. We call it a mistake, but in reality it is only a lesson. We have learned what not to do. Sometimes, God takes these so-called mistakes and transforms them into something very positive. Those are the stumbling blocks that can become stepping stones. It depends on how we use them. Regardless of how high we rise, we must keep our feet on the earth/ ground to keep ourselves in balance.

All we have to do is to know that the Power — the unconditional love — lies within all of us and is with us always. We can overcome every problem. It is all up to us to choose the right path.

Life is constantly changing and evolving. If we make bad choices, and it seems that there is no way out, have faith and know there is something better around the corner. It is simply that we have to remove the old that no longer serves our purpose and open the door to something better. To live means to grow and to grow means to change. Most of us fear change, but we must embrace it and love it and have patience to rebuild the new on the old foundation, using the wisdom gained from previous experiences. The best way to go through life is to stay open to everything, attached to nothing. Since everything is temporary, enjoy it while it is yours. Remember that the decisions we make are the doorways that will lead us to God – the light – or to the darkness. We have the freedom to choose. It's all up to us.

When we surrender our will to God, we let God light our way. If we have good intentions, God is on our side. Have faith. As I look at my first husband's life, I understand why he was behaving the way he did. He was taken to the army as a very young, innocent man and trained to kill people just as innocent as he was. He was wounded and lived with a bullet lodged in his thigh for many years, limping — in constant pain. Maybe the alcohol soothed his physical and emotional agony, but at the same time it was destroying his physical health and his life. Maybe, because of his addiction to alcohol, the school authorities were hesitant to ordain him as a priest. Then, when they reconsidered, he was no longer sure that he wanted to become a priest. God is nonjudgmental.

Apparently the Power – God – wanted to prove to us that nothing is all good or all bad. Therefore, God used Gerard's seeds to create three wonderful bright, loving, giving and very caring children. All three are dedicated to helping others to have better lives. Now, our grandchildren are also trying to make this world a better place. The Power, God, likes to create heroes in adversity. The truly great Spirit becomes more visible in times of disaster. Since God is Light; God shines brighter in times of darkness.

From the moment I stepped on US soil, it was like heaven had opened up. People treated me like a celebrity. Reporters surrounded me, asking me questions. People greeted me and wanted to know a lot about me. Some of them asked if I was an actress. One businessman bought me lunch. Great opportunities were coming my way, but I didn't take advantage of them. I am writing this so that people who read my story will learn from it.

After I became a cosmetologist, my patrons were very generous. They showered me and my children with gifts. They invited me to dinners in their homes or clubs and tried to introduce me to some single men. Many men wanted to marry me, but I was reluctant to try again. I enjoyed my freedom. The men were very kind to me. We would go to nightclubs for dinner and dancing or to concerts and operas. After the concerts, we were often invited to dine with the conductor and the stars. I had the privilege of meeting many talented artists. Life was very interesting.

I was working very hard without any vacations, trying to save money so I could take my children with me to Rome, Italy. They were in private schools, but I have always believed that travel is very educational. From the time my oldest daughter, Miriam, was seven years old, Elizabeth was five and Renee was three, they were all taking private lessons in French and piano. Polish, my native language, was taught in parochial school by Felician nuns and spoken at home. Later, my girls took dancing and formal voice lessons so they would have a well-rounded education and appreciate the arts.

They are all very talented. From the age of four, Miriam, the oldest, participated in the city's youth theater program. At her first performance, playing three different roles — a flower, a mushroom and an Asian child — Miriam stole the show. Children always do, because they are themselves and there are no expectations on our part. She made mistakes, but people enjoyed it. At one point, she came off the stage and was looking for me. I was expecting it, so I stood at the entrance door. She could not see me, so she went back on the stage. Then when the children finished singing, Miriam continued to sing. So the orchestra continued to play. The audience became quite excited. Then Michigan Governor Milliken, who was sitting in the first row, was very impressed by her. After the performance, he went onstage, picked her up to the microphone and asked her to say her name. The next day, the producer called me to tell me that he was getting a lot of calls from people who were impressed with her talent.

Elizabeth and Renee also started to perform at the age of four and continued through high school. They are talented in many arts. From a very early age, I used to take them to concerts, ballet and operas. In High School, they took art lessons. I wanted them to experience and appreciate different forms of art. Now, I know that when they retire they will never be bored. It is good to have hobbies.

It is also important to travel, and that's why I made the decision to take the children to Italy. It was an amazing experience. We stayed at the Metropol Hotel and the manager not only admired my girls, she catered to them. The master chef prepared special meals for them. We went sight-seeing and to the opera and museums. Through a priest in our parish in Detroit, we had a pass to visit the Vatican Museum. While there, a Cardinal escorted us through portions that were not open to the public. We saw the Pope's private chapel and many of the Vatican treasures and relics, including the skulls and bones of famous saints. My then eight-year-old daughter, Renee, had to use the bathroom and was allowed to use the Pope's toilet — escorted by the Cardinal since no woman is allowed inside. On Easter Sunday, we went to the Vatican for Easter Mass. There were approximately 100,000 people and, somehow, my youngest daughter became separated from us. We were all desperately trying to find her, but could not. I finally told my other daughters, "Maybe we should stay where we are and she will find us." Sure enough, after a short time, she did come to us with another girl. We were all so happy that there was no harm done.

Then we went to the Basilica and the Sistine Chapel to see Michael Angelo's paintings and sculptures. Every day, we visited different parts of old Rome. It was very educational and pleasant. We even went to the Opera House to see the performance of "Il Due Foscary," which is rarely performed outside of Italy.

Two days after we returned to Detroit, I received a telephone call from Richard Konefke, a man I had never met. One of my clients had given him my telephone number and suggested he call me for a date. But since I had decided not to date anymore, I told him that I had just returned from Europe and was very busy. I had never spoken to anyone quite that abruptly before. I was sure he would never call me again. But, after a week he called me again. I was very surprised. Then I asked him if he was a traveling salesman. When he assured me he was not, I decided to have dinner with him. He was very pleasant, but when we said, "good night," I thought that would be the end of it. A few days later, I received flowers and a telephone call inviting me to dinner again. That day, he asked me to marry him. I told him that we should wait.

During our courtship, Richard would come and sit on the floor and play with the children or take them to play tennis. The two older daughters liked him, but my eight-year-old was not so sure. Every few weeks, he would ask me if I had made up my mind, but I was trying to postpone my decision. I noticed certain things that made me wonder. He had told me that he wasn't a traveling salesman, but he traveled frequently on the job and had a company car. I wondered if he was telling me the truth.

Lesson: When there is doubt, leave it out.

But my children, especially my middle daughter, kept saying, "We want a daddy." Then one day, I asked my children to choose between a wealthy older gentleman, who had also proposed to me, and the younger poor one. Of course, they chose the younger one. I had certain reservations, but I was trying to make my children happy. I decided to marry Richard, thinking that, after all, no one is perfect.

One very stormy evening, he called me, very upset that he did not have enough money to buy me an engagement ring. I suggested he just buy the wedding band. He became extremely angry. I got scared and told him to forget about the wedding. Then I started to think, here is a thirty four- year-old young man with a degree in electrical engineering, living with his parents in a small apartment, driving a company car. Where was his money going? Suddenly, before one o'clock that morning, amid thunder and lightning in pouring rain, he showed up at my door. I let him in, and he started to apologize. So I forgave him.

One Sunday, he took me to meet his parents. They were very kind, but I sensed that the mother would have preferred someone without children. I understood that. The father was all for our marriage and said, "She will make a man out of him." As I look back at our marriage, I agree. I helped him to become more successful, and he helped me with my children by being a good father. They loved him. Apparently, that was our destiny. After all, we are supposed to help one another and make a statement with our lives. So I am grateful for that.

A few months later, we got married. After our evening reception, we left for our honeymoon. He didn't tell me where we were going. I guess he wanted to surprise me. We were on the road for several hours when we suddenly wound up in a wooded area. He admitted that he was lost; It was close to four o'clock. So I said, "Let's sleep in the car, and we'll finish the trip in the morning." But he decided to find a hotel. After a while, we arrived at the hotel in London, Canada, and in the morning we started back on our way to Stowe, Vermont. The area and the weather were beautiful.

The next morning, when I woke up, my husband surprised me with breakfast in bed. That was very nice of him, and I was very grateful because it was the first time in my life I'd had a husband do that for me. God bless him. He had a rather sensitive and romantic nature. I liked that about him. The weather was nice and warm, so we went swimming and took a walk. As we ate dinner at the motel, the owner stopped by our table and asked me if I was a movie star. He explained that he had never had such a beautiful woman staying in his motel before. I told him, "no," and thanked him for the compliment, but I noticed that my husband was jealous. He could not tolerate it if anyone, man or woman, complimented me. I tried to overlook that and enjoy our trip. The next day, we went to the Von Trappe Family Lodge for dinner in Stowe. There, we met Mrs. Von Trappe. She sat down and talked with us. After dinner, we visited her store, and I bought her book, "Maria." Then we visited the graves of her husband and one of her children, both of whom are buried on their property. The next day, we went to Mount Mansfield then visited Burlington and the Shelburn Museum where Grandma Moses' paintings are featured. It was a wonderful experience.

As we drove home, I tried to take pictures of the beautiful scenery in Vermont. I was excited about sharing so much beauty with my husband. Suddenly, he became very angry. I didn't know what had happened. When I asked him, he said, "If you would have to leave this place, you would be angry too." I said, "I am with you, we're both leaving … let's enjoy it while we can." But, I knew that there was more to it than that.

Lesson: Travel helps us to see what we see better from afar.

When we arrived home, we started to look for a house near good schools and universities. In a short time, we found a house in a nice location for a great price. His parents gave him $5,000 toward the down payment and I pitched in the rest. I bought the furniture, so in October of 1968 we moved in. Our first holiday together was very pleasant. We even decided to have a New Year's party in our house. I cooked and baked, trying to please everybody. There were eighty guests — friends, relatives and patrons. We all had a very good time and everything went well.

Shortly after the holidays, my husband's mother had a heart attack and died. The day after the funeral, his father had a heart attack and was taken to the hospital. After a week or so, he called us and spoke to me. He sounded cheerful, happy that he would be coming home the next day. "We are going dancing," he said jokingly. The next day, we got a call that he had died.

It was very hard on all of us. After the division of inheritance, my husband brought home twelve thousand dollars from life insurance policies, some stocks and five thousand in cash. I never asked how much money was in the estate. He told me that most of the money went to his sister, perhaps, because she had three children. After all, I didn't marry him for his money. My children wanted a daddy and he was their choice. I was willing to tolerate his imperfections as long as my children were happy. They came first.

Lesson: There is an old saying, "If mother is happy, the family is happy." Instead, women tend to try to please others rather than themselves.

However, I started noticing sudden shifts in his personality. Sometimes, his moods would change abruptly for no apparent reason, and he would make the children cry. But life is not perfect, nothing is. I am very grateful that he participated in my children's lives and never refused to take them along wherever we went. (Now I realize that was not wise. No matter how long people are married they should never stop dating, spending time with each other.)

A few months after his parents' deaths, he decided to take the whole family on a lavish vacation. I tried to talk him out of it, but he insisted. In June, 1969, we went to Switzerland. The trip was very educational. We rented a car and traveled across the country. The weather was beautiful and we were constantly in awe of the dramatic landscapes. We landed in Montreux, a beautiful town near Lake Geneva where we visited historical sites. Then we went to Lucerne, Zurich, Appenzell, Gallen and Brintz. As we drove through the cities and playgrounds, we noticed how immaculate everything looked. The people everywhere were also very cordial.

My daughter, Elizabeth, celebrated her twelfth birthday in the restaurant in the Landhaus Motel, located on a higher elevation with trees, flowers and peacocks decorating the grounds. At dinner in the motel, the people at the next table sent her a birthday cake, and the musicians sang and played for her and even gave her a copy of their records. This made her birthday away from home very special and memorable.

When we arrived in Appenzell, and I asked a random lady on the street for directions to a store we were looking for, she went out of her way and took us all directly to the shop. She was extremely helpful. From Appenzell, we went to Lucerne where we visited museums and land that was preserved for people to see how life must have been like before and after the Ice Age. From Lucerne, we went to Brintz where I bought some handmade memorabilia, including beautiful tablecloths. Overall, the trip was enchanting. We were very grateful for the opportunity to see the breath-taking country and to all the people that greeted us like family.

A few months after our vacation, the company that my husband worked for gave all employees a psychological test. He told me he did not pass the test, and he lost his job and the car. I suggested he start his own business. I bought him a car and gave him some money to start the business. He invited another man to become his partner, but after a short time, the partner quit. So my husband hired some salesmen, and my children helped him in the office during the summer.

In the meantime, my husband found out that Dal Tile was looking for a manager for their warehouse in our area. The company hired him. Salary and a company car were included. This job did not require traveling, but he still traveled. Later, I realized why.

As a father, my husband was very helpful. When the children entered science competitions, we all were involved. They won awards every time. He built an above-ground swimming pool for them, and he loved to play with them. My children were in all-girl high schools, so when they had father-daughter dinner dances he was there for them. I am very grateful and so are my children for all he did for them. When we traveled, he realized that I took my children with me wherever we went, and he did not object.

But, again, his moods were peculiar at times. As they grew and matured and started to date, he felt that they were cheating on him. One time, he told me that he was going to find another family. I responded, "You think that the other children will not grow up and leave home?" He said, "Oh, no!"

He was always very jealous, acting very strangely. I felt like a yo-yo. I told him, "One minute you love me, the next you look at me as if you don't know who I am." I tolerated his mood swings because he was such a good father to my children.

About one year after we came home from Switzerland, I felt exhausted and weak. Finally, my customers insisted I see a doctor and sent me to Dr. Klein. He discovered that I had three nodules on my thyroid gland and advised surgery to remove them. He sent me to Dr. Altman, who performed the surgery.

On my first day back to work after my surgery, someone broke into our house and robbed us of all of our valuables. The morning before, after Richard had left our bedroom to go to the bathroom, I saw a short, mulatto man walk right into our bedroom. I sat up, frightened, and then he disappeared. It was a vision that I did not understand at the time. The next day, when we were robbed, four neighbors saw a man that looked exactly like the man in my vision carrying luggage out of our home. But they did not realize what was happening.

At two o'clock in the afternoon, the robber arrived at our house in a yellow taxi. He left with loaded suitcases. The neighbors thought that the man must have been a taxi-driver helping my husband with his suitcases as he was leaving town, so they did not call the police. When the children returned home from school, they found the house ransacked. Drawers were pulled out of dressers, their contents strewn across the floor, and beds. Closet doors were left open with dresses, shirts and coats on the floor. They called me as soon as they realized that we had been robbed. I almost fainted when I heard the news.

When I came home, I realized that everything of value that I had owned — jewelry, fur coats and my suitcases — was gone.

The shock triggered my thyroid to become overactive. I was very weak. People who have this problem often had to be hospitalized for up to three months (in those days). People didn't believe me when I told them that, throughout this ordeal, I worked everyday. I drove to work slowly using both feet on the brakes to be certain that I could stop on time. I ate more than ever, but felt weaker and kept losing weight from the diarrhea. The food flowed right through me. I was losing hair everywhere, including my eyebrows. I was so weak, I could barely lift my fork. I don't know how I survived. It just shows you that if we have to, we can do the impossible.

Finally, I went back to Dr. Klein who diagnosed hyperthyroidism. He treated me with radiated iodine to kill the gland that was killing me. He felt I was already too weak to survive another surgery. The treatment worked, but from then on I became hypothyroid and needed synthetic thyroid hormones to survive.

But, as I said earlier, God has a way of turning sad situations into happy endings. To build something new, we must remove the old. I found out that I was covered for $10,000 under our homeowner's insurance. The loss was over $15,000, but I was grateful for what the insurance paid me.

Shortly after, one of my patrons returned from a trip to the Orient. She gave me the address to a jewelry wholesaler and I started to import good jewelry. I sold it to my friends for a small profit, to give everybody the opportunity to own real gems for a reasonable price. One businessman, who returned from a Hawaiian vacation, where he had priced an opal and diamond ring for $1,600, saw my large opal and diamond ring for $400. He commented, "Regina, do you realize that you are selling for less than wholesale prices?" Of course, he bought the ring for his wife and gave it to her for their wedding anniversary. So I was happy that they were happy. By helping others, we benefit as well. We can turn tragedy into success. When gold went to eight hundred an ounce, and the import tax went up, I discontinued importing, but I was able to give to my children more than I planned originally. I was able to save the profit from the jewelry sales for my children's education.

At the same time, I started to make my own skin cream and lotion. I never thought to sell them. But one time, one of my clients asked me, "What are you using for your skin?"

I said, "I do my own thing."

She said, "You are so selfish. I want it too."

So, I gave it to her to try. She liked it, so other patrons started to buy it. They named it miracle lotion because it helped to heal and prevent the skin from blistering after sunburns. When my mother developed skin problems on her arms from her wrists to her elbows, and her skin began to look like a crocodile's, I took her to a dermatologist. He gave her some medication. After ten days, she called me and told me that the medicine didn't help. Then she asked, "Why don't you do something for me?"

I thought to myself, *"What does she think I am?"* Then, I sat down on the chair in my studio and prayed for guidance. That's when an idea came into my mind. I went and added more vitamins and delivered it to my mother the next day. After ten days, my mother called me, saying, "Do you know what happened?" I feared that I would be blamed for whatever had happened, but instead, my mother said, "That rough skin is all gone!" I suggested that she continue to apply the cream because the damage was deep. The problem was cured and never came back.

Lesson: What we are looking for is in us or at our doorsteps.

As time went on, the children graduated from high school and started to attend university. Miriam, my oldest, went to the University of Detroit. The other two, Elizabeth and Renee, attended Wayne State University, also in Detroit. They were all very good students. The oldest and the youngest had partial scholarships and the middle one had a full scholarship. During the summer, they continued to work for my husband, in his offices (at Dal Tile and his own side-business). All three girls also worked part-time at the University.

I continued to work four days a week as a cosmetologist, trying to support my family and save some money for our retirement. From the time we got married, I never felt secure. My husband was spending more than he was making. In the seventeen years we were married, I did not see any profit from his own business, the one I had helped him start, which he continued to run on the side. Whenever I asked where the money was going, he would reply, "What do you think I am living on?" I did not understand.

"You are living here with me," I said.

From the very beginning of our marriage when we moved to our house, we opened a checking account. I had my charge cards and Visa; He had an American Express card. I was always paying my bills in full and before the due date. So, my husband asked me to do the book keeping for the household. He would take a check or two from the book and write it to cash. So I never knew where that money was going. When I would ask him for the amounts, he would give me much smaller amounts than they were in actuality. At the end of the month, the bank statement often showed we were $250 short in our checking account. When I asked him why he was doing this, he said, "It is not important."

I answered, "When we are dealing with money it is important."

On more than one occasion, his American Express charges were more than he was actually making. Often, I had to add my money to meet his expenses. I always bought the food and took care of all of my children's needs from my own salary. The bonuses that he received from his job (as much as $3,000 every one to two months) always managed to disappear. He would always intercept the mail so that the money never made it to our account. I never knew where the money went, until much later.

One day, I decided to see a psychic woman. As she was looking at the cards, she asked me: "Do you have a husband?"

I replied, "Yes, I do."

"No you don't," she said. "Oh! There is another woman and children."

Only later did I realize that he was supporting another woman whose husband had custody of their children, and she did not work. It was clear to me, only then, where the money had been going. Still, I tolerated this, not filing for divorce while the children were still in college. I did not want to upset them. I just thought he was going through a change of life and this would pass.

Then, one day when he came home from Las Vegas, I noticed that he was wearing a wedding band that was not the one I had designed for him. When I asked him about the strange ring, he said, "I just like this cheap one."

But I knew what it meant and simply said, "You have to go where your heart is."

"Oh, no! I never cheated on you," he insisted.

"So where is the money going?" I asked.

"Oh, she never worked," he said.

I said, "No, she didn't have to. I did."

In April of 1983, a day before Renee's wedding, a person from Dal Tile Co. paid an unexpected visit because they had a problem reaching my husband and they were suspicious. When they found out he was traveling, they fired him. Again he had no job and no car. So I bought him a car because he needed to look for a job. After a short time, he found a job in Windsor, Canada. The job included a car, so I gave the car I had bought to my oldest daughter.

In 1984, I started the divorce process. One day before he came home, a woman from American Express called home and asked to speak to my husband because he owed over $2,000 on his charge card. When I told her that he was not home, she asked me, "Who are you?" When I answered, "I am his wife," she asked if my name was Loralynn. I said, "No." She immediately ended the conversation. When my husband came home, I told him about it and he quickly left the room. It turned out that he was building a house for a woman he had married in Las Vegas.

In the meantime, his first attorney quit, and he had to hire a new one. When I told my attorney about the incident, he wanted to put Richard in jail for bigamy. I said, "No." I knew that in three more months he would be free and if he lost his job over the conviction, it would be difficult to find another job with a criminal record. It would also likely destroy his new marriage. It would also prolong my case and cost me more money. Nobody would win. I just wanted to let him go.

Lesson: Love is not a beggar; it is a gift.

CHAPTER 7

VEILED BLESSINGS

Lesson: Don't dwell on what you don't have. Enjoy the things that you have and more will come.

In January, 1985, the divorce was final. A few days later, I went to the bank to take some money out so I could pay taxes on the house, but the teller told me that my husband had come in the day before and taken some money out. Only $1,000 remained. He had taken all of our savings in the United States and Canada, including our retirement savings — more than $40,000.

Later, Richard was sorry. He even told my daughter that he wanted to come back — but it was too late. I had learned my lesson. In May of 1985, he came to Miriam's wedding without his new wedding band and escorted her to the altar. At the reception, my mother asked him if he was married. He said, "No." When he was leaving the reception, I thanked him for coming and I told him how important it was to all of us to have him there. He started to cry so hard that he could not talk. The next day, Sunday morning, as I was leaving for church, he came and looked around and said, "Oh, nothing has changed." I noticed the ring on his finger and said: "So, you are married. Congratulations." And I let it go at that.

Three years later when Miriam gave birth to her first child, her son, Christian, Richard came to visit them, but only once. He kept in contact with Elizabeth and Renee for a while longer, but that fizzled out as well, despite their efforts to keep in touch with him.

By that time, I had become an accomplished artist. I had started to take art lessons in October of 1979. I knew that I could draw. I had done architectural and mechanical drawings. And at age twenty two, my friend, Bill, an architect who had seen some of my sketches of people, realized I had talent. Finally, with my children all in college, it was time for me to do what I enjoyed doing. It was now or never; I was going on fifty two years old.

Lesson: The biggest changes seem to come very suddenly, in a split second when we least expect them.

Around that time, Sister Ignatius, a renowned and respected local high school art teacher, retired and started teaching adults. I took art classes from her. My mother thought I was too old, and it was too late. But I insisted that, "As long as I am alive, it's not too late." Eight months later, I was commissioned to paint a large painting of a snow leopard for an architect. His wife ordered it for him as a Christmas present. I had only three weeks to do it. The painting was done in oil. She did not rush me, but I was trying to please her and I did. Some of the other students also started to buy my paintings.

In a year, I had two collectors, prominent business people, George Lukowski and the Awrey Bakery corporate owners (a husband and wife team). I was commissioned to paint the portrait of a Chrysler Corporation executive. Two years later, I had a one-woman show of seventy two paintings in a variety of media. A few months later, Shelby Gallery in Houston, Texas, was buying my art and selling it for 60% more. As time went on, I began competing on the local level. I had another one-woman show in the Orchard Lake College Gallery. Later that year, I was an artist by invitation at Manresa

Retreat Center. That helped me to add another collector, Milford Woodbeck, and to sell my paintings and prints. In 1988, I won first and fourth place at the Michigan State Fair exhibit. That same year I also won the Kubinski Award at the State Art competition sponsored by the Friends of Polish Arts. In 1987, 1988 & 1990, I entered national and international competitions and my paintings were winning certificates and money as well as gold and silver medals. I was featured in The Detroit News and suburban papers and magazines like The Philippine Times, USA Today, People Magazine, the Michigan Natural Resources Magazine (October, 1996), as well as television shows on Channel Seven News, Farmington TV and Cablevision.

After a few months of studying with Sr. Ignatius, who was teaching us to use pencil, ink and tempera, I branched out on my own to paint in oil, watercolor, acrylic and pastels. My first watercolor painting was of a pair of European finches. I loved their beautiful colors — the blue, pink and black. I sketched them and wet the paper, and as I started to drop the colors for the background to blend them, they started to blend on their own so fast that I moved away from the table, realizing that some other Power was doing this and it looked great! I thanked the Power (God) for helping me. It was like a miracle, and I finished the rest. The painting was in the National Audubon Art Show in Los Angeles in November 1987 and in many shows where it won certificates and money. I called it a miracle, but most would consider it a biophysical phenomenon.

A few of my paintings and sculptures were assessed by two art professors — Professor Todd from the Center of Creative Studies in Detroit and Professor Wilbert, from Wayne State University — as well as my own teacher, Sr. Ignatius, as "impossible." They asked me, "How did you do it?" I didn't ask anybody how to do it. I just did it, and it worked. I created a sculpture of Eve and a god of Peace, both standing sculptures made without any metal girders. I also fashioned a sculpture of the Polish eagle with open wings, also without any metal. The Polish Eagle, which was 26 inches tall with an 18-inch wing span, was commissioned by the Polish Cultural Center in a suburb of Detroit. These pieces were displayed in many shows and admired by a few curators from different Museums during several critiques in our Farmington Art Club.

My teacher said, "It's no use to tell you it's not going to work, because you are going to do it anyway." I said, "Yes, I will try." After I finished the work, they would admire it and admit, "It works!"

Lesson: We should always try because nothing is impossible.

I made those kinds of mistakes when I was young. I was afraid to try. I remember a short time after I started to take art lessons, Daniel Green, a famous artist from Seline, New York, had a seminar at the Grosse Pointe Academy. I decided to take the class. I came with oil pastels, paper and the easel that I had at home. After he looked at my supplies, he told me, "Your pastels and your paper are all wrong. You need soft pastels and good paper for pastels, and the cardboard for back up is wrong." I figured since I had already paid for the seminar I would stay and do the best with what I had. Out of the blue, one of the artists gave me the soft pastels and the paper I needed. I thought, now I am in business. But the easel didn't work properly, so I decided to sit and paint. As we were painting the first model, Mr. Green was watching me, maybe because he realized that I was so inexperienced. At one point, he approached me and said, "Oh, I like what I see."

In the afternoon, we had to paint another model dressed as a drummer boy in Washington's army. After everybody was finished, Mr. Green came to me and offered his critique.

"I like what you did here," he said. Then he pointed to the fringe area and asked," But how did you do it?"

I said, "I didn't do it."

But he insisted, "I saw you do it!"

I said, "Yes, but I didn't do it."

I meant I did not know myself how I managed to capture all the details and make the linen look exactly like linen. Yet, every thread was outlined, and every stitch was there. The wool looked like wool, and the velvet looked like velvet. The class started to laugh.

One artist asked, "Mr. Green, you mean you are learning from your students?"

"Yes," he replied. "All the time."

> *Lesson: Do your best and the rest, leave to God. Every mystical experience is an intense, intimate and memorable one. We don't forget those.*

Another explanation for Mr. Green's surprise is this: He had no expectations. Having expectations leads to disappointment.

A few weeks after the seminar with Daniel Green, I received an invitation to include my art in the book titled, "Directory of American Portrait Artists." I was honored, but at the same time, I avoided it and, ultimately, refused. I was new in the field of art; I did not even try to apply. That was wrong. We should always try. Another artist, who was in that class with me, entered and was accepted.

> *Lesson: We are never sorry that we tried and failed, but we do regret when we didn't even try.*

The public thought I was good enough, but I did not believe in my own talents enough. It seems that every decision based on fear is wrong. As I was entering a lot of shows and winning, people were buying my art and commissioning me to paint specific paintings. I paint in all media and styles — realism, surrealism, abstract — and I also sculpt. I was able to satisfy many people. I was also invited to be a motivational guest speaker for organizational functions. In 1987, my painting was featured in the National Audubon Society Art show. In March 1996 and 1997, my paintings were winners in the Michigan State Wildflower competition and toured with the other winners throughout the state's museums and Art Centers. My paintings were also in International shows in 1987, 1988 and 1990 held in Los Angeles, Hollywood and Las Vegas. The shows were looking for artists who work in more than one category. I presented five categories and all had to be well-done. I won gold or silver medals in all five categories.

In May 1998, I was awarded two Merit awards in two different shows for a pencil portrait titled, "Sisters." In 1999, I was nominated and awarded the lifetime title of Deputy Governor of the American Biographical Institute Research Association. My art work is also in the Archives on Women Artists in the Library and Research Center in the National Museum of Women in the Arts in Washington, D.C.

In 1986, I became an owner of "Regina's Fine Arts." Some of my work is still available in limited edition prints. Since 1999, I have been included in 'Who is Who of American Women,' 'Who is Who in America' and 'Who is Who in the World' in the International Biographical Center in Cambridge, England, and in the Biographical Institute publications. In September 1998, my painting of Diana, Princess of Wales, entitled, "I Care," was accepted as part of the permanent collection by the Althorp Museum in Northamptonshire, England. Many of my paintings are in private homes throughout the United States, Canada, England, Poland, the Philippines, India and Austria. My art has been shown and sold in several galleries, including: Shelby Gallery in Houston, Texas; International Gallery in Bloomfield Hills, Michigan; Ambleside Gallery in Grosse Pointe, Michigan, and in DuMouchelles Art Galleries in Detroit, Michigan.

I am very grateful for my teachers, collectors and all the people who supported me from the very beginning, including Mr. and Mrs. Awrey. Mr. Irving Dubrinski, a businessman who was my very first collector, commissioned me to paint eight historical paintings in pencil of Greektown in Detroit. He had prints made and distributed them to schools. Two of these paintings were in the international competition in the ethnic category and won gold medals. George Lukowski, a businessman, commissioned me to do sculptures of him and his wife. He also bought some of my paintings. Milford Woodbeck, another successful businessman, collected my work until the day he died.

Joseph Bianco, who was a passionate art-lover, bought and commissioned a lot of my paintings. I was very honored to be among the great renaissance artists — millions of dollars-worth — in his collection. He was a true lover of art, a man who had big dreams. When he had a fire in his business (he was dealing in plastics) I learned that plastics don't produce flame, but smoke. The Insurance Company chose me to do the restorations. I had been restoring art for other artists in my neighborhood, for the University of Detroit-Mercy High School and Sarah Fisher Homes. I repaired holes in canvases and restored frames and sculptures.

But the Bianco repairs were the most ambitious restorations I had ever done. As I was working in his offices, another artist was working to restore the walls that Bianco had imported from Europe. They were carved from wood and two stories tall.

The artist observed me as I restored the wooden frames on the expensive paintings as well as the canvases that were damaged. He watched me for a long time. Then he came to me and said, "If you can do this, you can do anything. I am retiring after this project. I would like you to have all my supplies." And he kept his promise. He gave me all sorts of chemicals I later used to restore damaged ornate wooden frames for other facilities and artists.

Bianco had chosen me for the project because he had already collected my paintings and knew my skills. I was challenged by the project but did not know how much to charge for my work. I was very reasonable, but this was an extremely big job. The paintings were worth millions of dollars. The voice inside of me said, "Call the adjuster," but I did not do it, thinking that maybe he would not be allowed to help me. As a result, my bill was too low. It was so easy for me to do it, that I was afraid to charge a lot.

The adjuster and my collector asked me, "Why so little; what is wrong? You could have retired for the rest of your life on what you could have earned on this job!"

Lesson: Do not ignore your inner voice; Listen and push away the fear.

Every mistake I ever made was because of fear. God is very patient with me and all of us. He knows that we have to learn how to walk through life. God gave me a lot of talents; these were my tools. He knew I would need them all — and I did.

There is no end to creativity. Every necessity is hustling our creativity. After I came to the United States, I started to knit, do needlepoint, sew dresses and make hats for my family and myself. From an early age, I watched my mother who was very creative. Both of my parents were creative and handy. That's why we survived the war and revolution.

God provides us with all we need before we are born. It is up to us to use all the gifts, and share with the rest of the world. God loves givers because He is using them to spread His goodies throughout the world. In giving, we are truly receiving, and it makes us feel good and important. Never worry where the money or things that you want to give will come from. I live like that. All I do is tell God what I would love to do or give, knowing that He will provide — even if it takes being robbed. After all I had was stolen, in a short time, people helped me to get back all I needed and more. I was able to give to my children and grandchildren more than before and even help other people. All we need is faith.

CHAPTER 8

FLASHBACKS

Lesson: We are looking for perfection. What we call perfection, the straight line, is boring. I admire the crooked branches and crooked trees.

As I reflect on my past, I see many examples of guidance, destiny and even circumstances that seem eerily similar. For instance, the first time I arrived in New York City had special significance. Little did I know that thirteen years later, I would make another trip there and have an experience that was almost déjà vu. Just like my first day in America, people were receptive and kind.

It was November 18, 1962 and I was visiting New York to attend the Paderewski Foundation Ball at the Plaza Hotel. Again, I received a very warm welcome. At the ball, people named me "The Flower of Poland," maybe because I was wearing a white dress and a red velvet cape — the colors of the Polish flag. The porters carried my suitcase, but didn't want my money, saying, "Thank you, it was my pleasure."

Jan Kiepura and his wife, Marta Eggert, both opera-singers, were at the main table with other dignitaries, signing their photos. I was able to secure their photo and speak to him. The next morning,

Kiepura called me to say that his wife told him that she had seen a lot of beautiful women in her lifetime, but nobody like me. That day, I decided to go to the United Nations Building. When I was in the taxi cab, the driver asked me where I wanted to go. When he realized that I was not from New York, he offered to show me the city without extra charge because he could use his lunch hour to do so. I agreed. After he took me to the United Nations, he asked me when I would be leaving New York because he wanted to take me to the airport. So I told him the details.

On the way back to the hotel, I stopped to have lunch in a nearby delicatessen. It was crowded, but I was not in a hurry, so I joined the line. People who were on a time schedule asked me to let them go first, so I did. Suddenly, a lady came to me and said, "We are watching you standing in the same spot and letting everybody go ahead of you. I just finished eating, there are four of us, so you may take my place. Come with me."

When I went to the table, there were two ladies and a gentleman. He asked where I was from. I told him, Detroit, Michigan. He replied, "Oh, you are my lands woman. Anything you want is on me." He paid for lunch, and I thanked him. We had a very nice afternoon.

> *Lesson: The more we give the more we receive. The universe*
> *likes givers because it is anxious to keep on giving.*

When I returned to the hotel, I found a note from Colonel Leo Dulacki who was sitting next to me at the ball and with whom I was dancing the night before. It was not clear if he was inviting me to lunch or dinner. I looked at the clock, and I thought that, by now, he was already eating somewhere. I did not answer because I had another invitation to go to the theatre. The next day, I had lunch with Professor Domaracki and learned that the invitation had been for dinner. He told me that everybody had been talking about me, The Flower of Poland. They said I looked like an actress.

Professor Domaracki had proposed to me ten years earlier when I had first arrived in the US and was only twenty two. Now he was married and he and his wife had lost their only child as an infant. Still, he asked me again why I had not married him. He really loved me. I did not answer then, but now I think it was because it was necessary for me to experience all that I did to become the woman I am today.

The day I was leaving New York, the porter took my suitcase down and as I was trying to pay him, he said, "No thank you, it was my pleasure." When I was waiting outside to meet my taxi driver, another man walked over to me and asked if my name was Regina. I told him it was. He explained that his friend was busy and asked him to take me to the airport. I thanked him. It was very nice of him to do that. As we arrived, he took my suitcase and carried it into the building. When I paid him I included a tip, but he wouldn't accept the tip! My story is very unusual. I have nothing, but good memories about New Yorkers.

Lesson: Tomorrow we get out of the river of life what we put in today.

When I became a cosmetologist and started to work, I did the same thing. People were giving me tips and I said, "No, thank you." Many times, I didn't charge for some extra work — until one time, when the owner saw what I was doing and called me into her office. She said, "I don't know where you come from, but on this earth we need money. How are you going to support your children and how am I going to stay in business?" I presume, if you love what you do, and do it with love, you don't think about what is in it for you.

CHAPTER 9

A NEW ERA OF
SPIRITUAL VISION

Lesson: Humans too — the more scars and wrinkles they have, the more they shine like a gem. Each scar and wrinkle has a story. Even stars in the sky have scars.

Everything we go through is a lesson that brings out our talents. It forces us to think and create in order to survive. I call it cutting the facets in a diamond. When a diamond is freshly excavated, it doesn't shine as much. After the facets are cut and the matrix is removed, that's when it begins to shimmer.

And so it is with us. We are born gems in the rough, and life has to cut out the facets. That's how we develop compassion, and our souls start to glow. As we grow older, we become more beautiful because that is what true beauty is — a reflection of the lessons learned by the soul. We have been led to believe the contrary, that beauty fades with age. But, the truth is, our souls (which contain our true beauty) never get old. As we age, we grow better just like everything else in nature, just like good wine.

These are the messages and kernels of wisdom that will be embraced even more as the earth shifts, and we enter a new era of thinking. In this new era, the collective consciousness of society will be less focused on the three dimensional world and more on the multi-dimensional realm of the spirit. We will see more with our minds instead of our eyes.

We will push back the stones in our lives with greater ease because we will understand that the stone is not really there. It is just an obstacle, a piece of matter placed in front of us by a mind that is stuck in a rut of complaining and believing in powerlessness. As we become more spiritual, we will recognize the spirit as the true source of all of our strength. I say this because I have a doctorate degree in life, and that's a wider scope of knowledge.

My knowledge is the result of both the hardships and the spiritual experiences that started surfacing in my life when I was ten years old. Back then, the spirits began coming to me suddenly and clearly. To this day, they appear without being invited. I see them in the daytime or in bright light or in dreams. Every vision is different, so they still stun me. Many times, I have to guess their message and the activities continue until I do.

Lesson: Being spiritual means knowing the ultimate source from which all things come — The Universal Mind (God).

Sometimes, the spirits speak to me like my father did. The day my father died I had a vision at seven thirty in the morning (before he actually took his last breath). I saw him walking in a beautiful garden with his shorts on — without a walker. I said, "Oh, you are walking and you have no pain?"

He turned around, looked at me and said, "Pain? … No," and walked on.

I was in Texas helping my daughter, Renee, to move. When she woke up I told her what I had seen and said, "I think that Grandpa is dying, or he died and came to say good-bye." At nine o'clock in the morning, Texas time, the telephone rang. My daughter, Elizabeth, who was helping my parents, was on the line telling us that Grandpa was home from the hospital but not doing well. He was not alert and was breathing strangely. A nurse was coming to help care for him. Then she handed the phone to my mother so she could go to check on him. As I spoke to my mother, Elizabeth interrupted to report that she had watched Grandpa take his last breath.

Three weeks later, my mother told me that my father came in the morning with another man and was looking for their dog, Ali. A week later, she had to put the dog to sleep.

The next time my father came to me was in the afternoon as I was resting on the sofa in the living room of my home. Suddenly, I saw my father walking from the bay window. As he stood and looked at me, I reached for his hand and tried to kiss it, but my fingers went through his hand. Then he walked away through the window. It seems that what we see in the spiritual world is not corporal.

After my father died, my mother sold their house and came to live with me. Nine years later, my mother died. She lived like an angel and died like an angel, walking and talking to the very end. She came to me in my dreams many times. When I was working on a prophetic painting, Pavarotti came to me in my dream with some young English nobleman. Another time, Princess Diana was sitting and smiling at me but as I extended my hand to greet her, she pulled her body back as if to avoid touching me; To touch me would mean I would join her in death soon. At that time, I was working on her portrait, "I Care." I received her message, "It's okay. Finish it." The painting is now in the Althorp Museum in England.

Lesson: Be true to yourself. God has placed the truth in your soul.

It seems to me that the people or animals who love us, or whom we have helped while they were alive, become our guardian angels after they die. My music teacher, Helen Hopkins, came to me twice. The first time, it was Sunday, Mother's Day. I made a reservation for a family dinner. That day, I received the call from Mrs. Hopkin's niece that she had died. I thought that the funeral would probably be in a day or two. When I came home from the dinner, I walked into my library and looked into my living room. I saw that the screen on my fireplace was open and pushed out. I thought that some animal had fallen down the chimney and had pushed open the fireplace screen. I looked all over but did not find any animal. Then I decided to call her niece and ask when her funeral would be held. She told me Mrs. Hopkins had been cremated that day. Then I understood the message from the fireplace.

The next time, she came to me in a dream at 7:30 on the morning of June 6, 1995, two days before my daughter, Elizabeth, graduated from Harvard Medical School. She said, "My name is Helen. I am your guardian angel. God sent me to you to tell you that He does not want you to sacrifice for Him any longer. Go enjoy your life." When I woke up, I was thinking, *What did I sacrifice for God? For my children, Yes.* So I didn't change anything. This experience made me think that perhaps she became my guardian angel because I saved her from being raped by a young man once.

He had come to the door of her home in Highland Park, Michigan one afternoon when I happened to be visiting. By then, her neighborhood was pretty rundown with many homes boarded up. She answered the door despite my protests, because the young man looked so proper. He initially pretended to be looking for someone. He noted that she was elderly and lived alone. He did not see me in the other room where she kept her piano. He stopped her from shutting her front door and forced his way inside. He acted surprised and became more nervous when he saw me in the other room. He had not counted on dealing with more than one woman.

He led us both upstairs where he tied me up and shut me in her bedroom closet. Luckily, he was shaking so much that his knots were loose enough for me to work my hands free. The closet door was closed but not locked, so I let myself out and ran downstairs where he had taken Mrs. Hopkins. He was struggling to remove her clothing as she lay tied up on the couch. I ran out the front door, screaming for help. Even though the neighborhood was fairly deserted, the intruder became more nervous and ran away, leaving us both alive and essentially unharmed but traumatized. We filed a police report. After we identified him in a line-up, the police said he was eighteen years old and had committed similar crimes in the past.

Lesson: Silent spiritual force is stronger than physical force.

Over the years, I became close friends with a client and her husband, Dr. Altman. The Altmans and I would get together to talk, go out to dinner. We sometimes traveled to Northern Michigan for brief vacations along the lake. When Dr. Altman developed cancer, I would call him often to see how he was feeling and to offer words of encouragement. One day, I came home and noticed that the plant in the living room was moving rapidly, almost as if it was in the middle of a windstorm. I started to run and check where the wind was coming from. I could not find anything open. Then the wind stopped. So I walked out of the room. Then I turned around to check whether or not the plant was still. Suddenly, it started to move again. This time, I stood in the hallway and thought, *What is going on?* At that moment, it occurred to me that Dr. Altman was saying goodbye to me. As soon as I got the message, the wind stopped. The next day, I got a call that Dr. Altman had died.

Recently, a former neighbor, a collector of my art, died. I went to the funeral home to spend some time with his family and participate in a prayer ceremony in his honor. But I didn't go to the funeral. Maybe it was important to him for me to be there at the final moment. One week later, his spirit came to me at seven thirty in the morning. He didn't speak, but I got the message: "You didn't come to me so I came to you."

In today's world, the spirits communicate even on the telephone. It happened to me. My ex-husband, Gerard, who died in 1982, contacted me a few months later. It was eleven p.m. when my telephone rang. I looked at the clock, wondering who was calling me so late? When I answered, I heard his voice, saying, "Help me … Help me, I am in purgatory."

I didn't tell anyone, but a week later, my mother called me and said that she received a phone call from a man asking her for help, saying: "Help me. Help me …" My mother thought that it was some man who was in a disabled car and needed help. So she said, "I don't have a car, I can't help you." But the voice was persistent, saying, "Yes, you can." Then I told her of my experience. (That is a proof to me that purgatory is real). After that, my mother went to church and ordered a special Mass to be said for his soul. That same night, unusual things happened around her. Her clock was thrown to the floor, and her blanket was pulled off of her. It was as if the evil spirits were angry with her for her appeals to God to spare his soul. She became fearful and prayed. I guess the evil spirits fight for every soul.

One morning, Gerard came to my bedroom with a smile. I tried to scream, "No! No!" But he continued to come and scratched my stomach. It felt like an animal's claws at the time. Later, I developed pain in my stomach. Eventually, I developed a bleeding stomach ulcer that nearly killed me. After our divorce, he had warned my mother that he would torture us even after he died. We have to be careful what we say, because words are very powerful and so are our thoughts.

Lesson: Do not fear because the things we fear will become reality.

One of my clients, Mrs. Silverman, like any mother whose son goes off to war, was worried about his survival. He was only twenty one years old when he was drafted to fight in Belgium during World War II. As she feared, he never made it home. She was so grief-stricken, she could not work or sleep. For at least one month, she could barely move from her chair. She could not and did not care about herself or anyone or anything else. Finally, her husband jostled her back to recognizing that she was still alive and needed to continue to live. Mrs. Silverman was able to function but continued to grieve her son's death, crying and begging him to take her with him.

Finally, one Saturday morning, her son appeared to her wearing military pants but no shirt and said, "Mother you must let me go. You are keeping me away from my duty."

Just like any loving mother, she cried and said, "But I want to be with you."

He replied, "No, you have a big job to do here."

It was true. Soon after this, she learned that her daughter had been diagnosed with Multiple Sclerosis and needed her help. Her daughter had two children to raise. Mrs. Silverman went on to live a long time. She helped her family and many other people until the last day of her life — she was a true angel. That is why her son sent her that message that morning. The people we love, we must set free.

Lesson: Motherhood is one of life's most splendid blessings.

I used to say when a woman becomes a mother, she immediately becomes a doctor, nurse, teacher, priestess, psychiatrist and bottle-washer. When the child gets sick, the mother is the first to evaluate if she can cure the child herself or if the child needs a doctor. Then she is the nurse, taking care of the child. As time goes on, she is the psychiatrist guiding the child through adjustments to life here on earth. Then she becomes the first teacher, teaching reading, writing, arithmetic and many other things while preparing the child to be accomplished and independent. Through it all, she is a priestess, teaching the child about God and how to pray. Prayer is very important. It prepares us for the journey of life. Prayer fills us with faith and leads us to success.

In today's world, the role of a woman extends beyond the home. Being a mother is a tremendous job in itself. But in many cases, women today also hold full or part-time positions outside of the home. With all the pressures, it is harder to be beautiful, and yet the world around us will not excuse us women. One would ask, "What does it take to be a beautiful woman?" My answer would be: a many-splendored life.

When it comes to our children, mothers have intuitive and spiritual awareness. I have those intuitions all the time, but they were more prevalent when my children were young. At one point, when my children started to walk, I remember taking them to a very good, well-known shoe store, "Podezwa" in Hamtramck. I bought good leather shoes for them. Miriam wore her shoes until she outgrew them. Then when Elizabeth, the second child was starting to walk, I did the same thing. One morning, as I was dressing her, I reached for her shoes and discovered that the left shoe was missing. I looked all over and never found the other shoe. The same thing happened with my Renee. When they got married and moved to different states, I finally got the message: Miriam remained in Detroit. Elizabeth and Renee were the two who left. The spirits are very creative.

One time, a beautiful cat came to my door. He was black with a white bowtie-shaped marking at his neck, a white button on his chest and a larger white V on his stomach — the markings of a Maltese. I used to call him my Prince. I figured he belonged to someone, but I fed him and assumed he would return to his owner. As cold weather was approaching and he kept returning to my door, I decided to adopt him. When I took him to the veterinarian to be examined, the doctor told me that he had Feline Leukemia. But I made the decision to keep him anyway and named him, Sammy. He was a true prince. He never broke or spilled anything. Everyone who met him admired him. After eight years, I had to put him to sleep.

Two years later, I had a dream that Sammy was sitting at my side door. I said to him, "Oh Sammy, you are here!" At that moment, he changed into a black and white dog. The following morning as I prepared to leave home, I noticed that my side door had been left unlocked all night. Then I realized his message: "I was your watchdog all night!" Now I know that animals are also our guardian angels after they die -- especially the ones that were adopted or saved by us. They are very grateful and so are we.

Everything that God creates has a purpose, to help us to live a good life. God provides angels in all forms. One family hiding in a bunker from German invaders recalls how they prayed for an angel to help them elude German soldiers who were hunting down and killing people in their village. One man was disappointed when he saw that there was only a spider at the opening of their bunker, thinking, "I asked for an angel, and God sends a spider!?" Later, when Germans discovered the bunker, it was the spider's intricate web, unbroken, that kept the soldiers from bothering to investigate inside. The family inside actually overheard one soldier tell the other, "It must be empty … don't you see the spider web? If there were anyone using this, this web would be broken or not here at all!" The soldiers departed; the hiding family was safe.

Lesson: Love is the most important word.

My passion is to leave this place much better than I found it, where people live in peace and harmony. We must return to the one word God gave us to live by – LOVE. Words are not enough. We have to practice that one word, LOVE that stands on a foundation of respect and tolerance. These are free gifts. No one can change anybody. But we each can change ourselves and, thus, the world can change. It will become heaven on earth. Love is very powerful; It heals and brings success to any endeavor.

We can accomplish any task we desire no matter how big if everyone makes the effort to change themselves. Nobody can do it for us. The source of our happiness is within us. We must choose to be happy. The love we give is the love we get. Sometimes, the love we receive does not come from the same person to whom we give it. But love is what will lead us to peace in the world. Love heals. It is the only thing that can save us.

CHAPTER 10

THAT'S NOT A SCAR;
THAT'S A BEAUTY MARK

Lesson: Life is a credit card. Beware of what you charge. You will have to pay later.

I used to tell my children that tough times were wounds that formed scabs on the outside and beauty marks on our souls. In other words, there's no such thing as a scar — just signs of beauty, symbols of hope and emblems of inner strength. But it's up to us to look at our experiences in that manner. It's up to us to embrace the good with the so-called bad.

To do so is to honor our spirit. It means that we are looking within instead of looking without. The challenges in our lives sometimes linger because we are looking for God outside of ourselves. The Creator, God, is inside of us and in everything God created. The change has to come from within us as well.

I am eighty seven years old now, and yet I am still facing endings and new beginnings because in every ending there is the seed of a new beginning to challenge us and elevate us to a higher ground. Hard times are beneficial for our spiritual growth. They bring us to balance, help us become more creative, compassionate, loving, sharing and grateful. I still remember that was what occurred during World War II. People who hadn't talked to one another in years because of some disagreement actually became close friends, helping one another and loving one another. Unbelievable talents were discovered. New opportunities opened up and I realized how creative my parents and our neighbors were.

We survived because we took advantage of every opportunity and every moment. Life is like a river, constantly changing. We must relax and flow with the current. It is impossible to swim against the current and succeed. We have to go with the flow and even if the flow is going somewhere we don't like, we must hold on anyway and believe it will all work out for our good. Think positive no matter what, and things will turn around in God's time.

During the war, we actually had to learn to laugh at life. If not, it would have killed us. The people who survive the valleys are the ones who put a little humor into gravely serious situations. When we survive an ordeal and look back, we often find that it was not as serious as it seemed at the time. We laugh about it later, so why not laugh about it now? Life is a stage on which we all have a part to play. Sometimes, that part is a tragic comedy. Yet, the experience will mold us into wiser and better human beings.

When my grandchildren were small, I used to demonstrate this by holding a tennis ball. I would ask them "what will happen if I drop the ball on the floor?" Then I would drop it and explain to them that it did not rise very high because there was no force behind it. After that, I would slam the ball down on the ground very hard, so they could see it bounce to the ceiling. I would tell them that "the harder we fall, the higher we rise. Just make sure you don't stay down. Rise!"

Lesson: Our greatness is measured by the way we surmount challenges, and rise to the top.

To live means to challenge yourself or life will. Challenge creates a purpose. Purpose gives us strength to get up in the morning, elevates our spirit to divine Love, fills us with energy, and takes us to a sphere of timelessness. As it fulfills itself, Spirit opens the door to riches beyond our imagining. I believe that the spiritual renaissance which we are already experiencing will save civilization.

Surmounting challenges is easier said than done. Adversity doesn't come gift-wrapped. It is ugly and terrifying, and we feel tempted to give up. But that is okay. We are going to stumble sometimes. When that happens, change course and go around the obstacles. Conquer them with a smile, and use them as the building blocks for your next great adventure. Allow the fear to enter. Embrace it, and let it be the fuel that fires you up to succeed. There is no life without what we call "growing pains." Experiencing the "downs," helps us truly appreciate the "ups." Life is a school that never ends.

In the process, choose to be happy. Did you know that complainers are simply people who are afraid to be happy? They don't know how to enjoy life, so they spend their time condemning and criticizing others. That is the wrong road because it will never lead to anything worthwhile. Take the road that is embellished by your dreams and destined to help you fulfill a divine mission.

We all come to this world with an assignment, the necessary tools (talents) and freedom of choice. The universe respects our choices, but the results are our responsibility. Why not use these God-given gifts to help make this world a better place? Why not take advantage of every opportunity to make a contribution or do something kind? Why not develop the courage and tenacity to become all that you were meant to be? Why not exceed your own expectations, teach by example, and make everything you do a genuine labor of love?

People who are really inspired (in the spirit) believe in making a statement with their lives. Those people are on fire because they have purpose. They know who they are and where they are going. They don't use expressions like "I can't" or "I am too old." That is what makes you old – the belief that you are over the hill or unable to learn new things.

Growth is a process that never ends, at least not as long as we are still breathing. And knowledge is the one gift that we cannot truly give away. No matter how much we share with others, it remains with us and keeps on increasing. Think about it: No one ever complains about too much knowledge, but almost everyone says, "If I would have known better, I would have done better." So you see, there is no end to learning. There is always a place for improvement no matter how wise and accomplished one appears to be.

We are noble beings. If we think of ourselves that way we will continue to reach higher. I tell all children to act like princes and princesses in order to honor their minds, bodies and souls. I encourage them to carry themselves that way so that they will succeed. But that is only one of the reasons I give this advice. I also want them to understand that that is the only way to gain respect from the world. What we think of ourselves is important. The more we think of ourselves, the more we understand our connection to the higher power we know as God.

I always told my girls that God doesn't need our recognition. God knows God is all that is – the creator of all. So, when we recognize the power of God, we recognize our own power. The mind, located in our heart, is the most powerful, creative, limitless tool in our body. It is never wrong. But the mind is soft-spoken. That is why we must meditate to quiet our brains, and let the Mind guide us in making the right decisions. If everyone would meditate every day, we would have peace and love on earth. We could remove war from the planet by observing spiritual practices.

Spiritual practices help us to see beauty in everything that surrounds us. This is how it works: We see ourselves in everything we look at. If we are focusing on beauty that is an indication that we are feeling good about ourselves for we see the reflection of our own self image in whatever we are beholding. Therefore, when we compliment others, we are complimenting ourselves. So it's a double compliment. Every time I receive a compliment I say, "Thank you, but I am just a reflection of your beauty."

As we nourish our spirits, our connection to everything becomes more and more clear. We also begin to understand how to tap into God's universal power. We learn never to tell the universe what we don't want. Why? Because you will be sure to get it. The universe knows only one word – Yes. Place an order for what you want, and let it go. Be patient, and you will receive it. I know from my own experience.

When I first came to this country with only one suitcase, it seemed impossible to believe that I would one day own a home in a unique neighborhood in Detroit. I used to drive by this neighborhood when I was a single mother of three young children, working as a cosmetologist. I would envision myself living there. About nine years later, I was moving into a home in that neighborhood. Currently, I still live there and I thoroughly enjoy it.

> *Lesson: Everyone has dreams. Keep the dreams of your heart alive. Visualize living your dreams, and they will come true.*

Our world is like a beautiful, colorful puzzle, and we are an integral part of it. Every piece is essential. If one piece is missing, regardless of how small, the puzzle is incomplete. I urge everyone to know their own worth and realize that they are an important segment in this divine tapestry. But understand that none of it — not your home, your children, the car you drive – is yours. Everything you have is borrowed, so enjoy it while you can. Be willing to move through life open to all there is but attached to nothing. And be willing to teach and to learn from the little ones in your life, for they are brilliant souls. They don't remember the past, and they don't relate to the future:

> *Lesson: Be us as the little children that the world might finally grow up.*

Life is service. We all are servants to each other — part of a bigger puzzle where each piece, each task, is important and valuable. Everyone deserves respect because every job or service is equally important to complete the grand puzzle of Life.

As I grew older, I discovered a new way to ask God for what I want by thanking God before receiving from God, knowing that it is done. Knowing is true faith. It is stronger than believing. If I say, "I believe," there is doubt — maybe it will happen; maybe it won't. Every day, when I get up and I look at the morning sky, I say: "Thank you, God, for the glorious day." I walk away knowing that it is done and it is. When the weatherman is predicting a storm, I say, "Not here!" Yes, there is rain and wind, but no fallen trees on our block. Knowing that it is done, I say, "Thank you." The thoughts and words are very powerful, so be careful what you are thinking or saying. No matter what the circumstances or conditions are, God is in control. God is "I Am". God is in everything and everywhere. If we are struggling, "I Am" is the provider. I know from my own experience. When I was struggling financially, my mother noticed that the money seemed to multiply in my hands. And it still does.

I remember when my Elizabeth applied for a job as a reporter at the Detroit News and there were 400 students applying for the same position. She was concerned, but I said, "God can do anything." So she got the job and in a short time received a certificate of recognition as the best youngest reporter. Ten years later, she won another competition, the Rotary Scholarship to pursue post-graduate studies anywhere in the world. She selected Calcutta, India. There, she chose to "study" on the streets, doing volunteer work that lead to her interest in medicine. When she came back to Detroit, she completed her pre-med studies while continuing to work full-time as a news reporter. She ultimately applied and was accepted to Harvard Medical School – with some scholarship assistance to help fund her studies. I later received a letter from Harvard saying that it was the first scholarship granted in fifteen years. I always prayed, knowing that God would provide the best education for my children, and God did.

I remember I wanted to give $250 to my father for his birthday, but it was too much for my budget. So I decided to buy a Lotto ticket. I didn't know much about Lotto, so, when I was at the store, I asked the person behind the counter for some advice. A lady came over and told me to play the three numbers she gave me, but I changed one number. It was wrong. The numbers she gave me won. Only then did I realize that she was an Angel that God had sent to help me. I am writing this so no one will repeat my mistake. As I look back at this incident, I remember that the lady walked over to me and without me asking her for advice, gave me the three numbers that were winners. That's how God works. God likes to surprise us.

Lesson: Accept the advice the way it is given.

It's also best not to expect people to behave exactly as you do. For instance, I have noticed that if someone borrows something from me, it's best to give it to them because I will never get it back. Even if they insist they will give it back, it never happens. Once I accepted that, I could not be disappointed. One time, my boss borrowed my necklace and earrings. As I was giving the set to her, she said, "I will bring it back." I told her, "Just take it as a gift."

When she returned from the party, she told me that she lost one earring and was sorry. This had happened to me before. So I learned that I cannot lend things. I have to consider whatever I lend as a gift. But I can borrow things, and I will return them in better condition than I found them.

Lesson: Be a cheerful giver.

In February of 1988, I was visiting my parents, and I saw how their neighborhood was changing and becoming more dangerous. I told them that I wanted to help them by buying Lotto tickets because I heard that the jackpot was $10 million dollars. Without hesitation, I said, "This is mine!"

And my father said, "Okay." He gave me ten dollars to buy the tickets for him too. It was a difficult time for me financially, but I added ten of my own, so we had twenty dollars to invest. I didn't know much about Lotto, but I was willing to try. When I came home and was opening my mail, there was a letter with the prayer to St. Jude, who is known to help us in difficult times. I started to pray. I went outside into the cold February weather, thinking that maybe I could connect with God better by being surrounded by nature. I never prayed as hard as I did then — crying and praying.

When I went home, I put a little bell in my dining room and asked God to ring it in the morning to let me know if I should buy the tickets. When I went upstairs to sleep, I was thinking to myself, "Will I hear that little bell ring?" Then the thought came to my mind that God can do anything. That was faith. At five o'clock that morning, the doorbell rang. I got up thinking, who is coming to me so early in the morning? But then I heard the little bell ringing. I realized that it was God answering my prayer, letting me know that it was a good time to buy the Lotto tickets.

I was very grateful, and I promised myself to buy the tickets that day after work. But I was so very busy working until late, that I did not stop at the store. I assumed it was too late to buy the tickets by then. A year later, on February 27, 1989, it was announced on the news that one ticket won the $10 million but nobody came to claim the money. Then I realized, God must have set aside the ticket that was meant to be mine. God did more than I asked. God kept God's promise. I am the one who did not do my part. I had perfect partners. My mother, my father and I were praying for the money. Many other people would have benefitted from it. I have no one to blame but myself. I should have pushed away that negative thought and gone to the store to see if I could buy those tickets. Maybe that is how God was testing my faith.

Now, when I pray, I thank God before I even see any favor from God, knowing that it is done —that is true faith. God knows the proper time to answer our prayer. God is always there to help us. That is why God's name is "I Am." All we have to do is to surrender our will. Let go and let God. If things appear to be going wrong, but we continue to believe and have good intentions, God will step in to lead us to success.

Lesson: With prayer, the impossible becomes possible.

MY PRECIOUS CHILDREN

One evening after my daughters had become adults and were actively pursuing their careers, my middle child, Elizabeth, stopped by for a visit. As we talked, she began telling me about an amazing movie about the Holocaust. She had just seen the movie and proceeded to regale me with some of its horrific stories. That movie was "Schindler's List." After listening to Elizabeth for awhile, I gently explained that I didn't' need to see the film. "I had lived it."

Her eyes grew big, and I could tell she was shocked. I realized then that it was time to sit down with all of my girls and share more details about my past. They were amazed that I had survived such an ordeal and impressed that I had done so with such grace.

However, they are the true testament of my success. When you grow up with pain and struggle, you hope for something so much better for your children. Any parent will tell you that. I wanted my daughters to have wonderful husbands and prosperous lives filled with love, joy and peace. So far, I can say that all three have accomplished this goal, and I am pleased that they are doing so well.

They are proof that if you release bitterness from your heart, it won't trickle into the lives of those who follow you. It warms my spirit to see them living such productive lives and enjoying so many opportunities. They remind me of how far I have come. They also inspire me because they are the fruit of my unrelenting faith.

Indeed, they are proof that God turns scars into stars. In other words, my life is full of scars but my children and grandchildren became stars. I am very proud of my children and grandchildren, all of whom graduated from universities with honors and are now pursuing higher degrees or careers.

Miriam graduated from The University of Detroit, Suma Cum Laude in Journalism and Theater. After graduation, she started to work for the Royal Oak Daily Tribune as a journalist. In a few years, she switched to public relations and worked at Sinai-Grace Hospital for Dr. Bloom on his Project Hope. Then she worked as office manager and public relations at Dal-Tile. She used her many skills to do various jobs — copy writer at Crowley's, telecommunications supervisor of sales operations for MCI — before she eventually settled into a career working for various health insurance companies and facilities. She worked for many years as a manager and analyst at Blue Cross Blue Shield then became Director of Operations at Trinity Health. She worked briefly as Vice President of Independent Health in Buffalo, NY before becoming the director of the Physician Group at Wayne State University. She went on to become Vice President of the Physicians Group at WSU. She and her longtime husband, Christopher Bielski, an accomplished artist, also managed to raise two bright and talented children who have graduated from college. Her son, Christian, is pursuing a career in politics and her daughter, Elizabeth, is pursuing a doctorate in chemical engineering.

My second daughter, Elizabeth, had a full scholarship to Wayne State University. She graduated with honors in Journalism and worked as a reporter for The Detroit News in Detroit. She also spent several months working for USA Today in Washington, DC. When she traveled to Poland on a vacation, she interviewed Lech Walesa and wrote a series of articles about life in Poland under the last vestiges of communistic rule. Then she competed and won a Rotary Scholarship to study anywhere in the world. She chose

Calcutta, India. There, she volunteered in Mother Teresa's Home for the Destitute and Dying, Kalighat. She also volunteered with Dr. Jack Prager who ran a sidewalk clinic in Calcutta. When she returned to the United States, she decided to go to medical school. She was accepted to Harvard Medical School. I received a letter from Harvard saying that she received the 1st scholarship in fifteen years, because "poor people do not go to Harvard." Because she speaks several languages, she had the opportunity to travel to other countries, including the Dominican Republic, Gabon in Africa and La Paz, Bolivia, to practice medicine. She graduated from Medical School with a Humanitarian award. During her residency in Minnesota, she spent several months in Chiang Mai, Thailand, learning about various infectious diseases. She is now a family physician in North Carolina and is married to an Infectious Disease specialist, Dr. Bruce Israel. They are raising their son, Nicholas, who is still in elementary school. Nicholas was born with stars in his eyes. He is still young but full of promise.

Renee has a degree in nursing from Wayne State University. She took a five-year course which allows her to practice anywhere in the country. After she graduated and married Mark Gilchrist, they moved to Houston, Texas. There, she started to work as a nurse in Memorial Herman Hospital in their burn unit where she stayed for more than twenty years. She had to drive an hour each way to / from work but still calls it her "first love." She recently started to work as a nurse in Interventional Radiology closer to their home. She and her husband (a special task force police officer) raised two beautiful daughters, Jacqueline and Emily, who have graduated from universities in Texas and are now working in physical training.

My young stars sparkle and glow, despite the challenges of my early years. In fact, they shine because of it. You see, without the stormy days of my past, I wouldn't have developed so much wisdom, strength and determination. They are the products of the lessons I shared in this book.

They are the ones who will be carrying the torch for many years to come.

ACKNOWLEDGEMENTS

I want to express my ultimate gratitude to God for guiding and helping me through my life.

Without my grandparents, Wardach and Engelhardt -- who helped me and my family through the tough times and through the war -- we may not have survived. My parents, Maria and Marian Engelhardt, never stopped loving and helping me and my family in innumerable ways. My only brother, Mitchell, and especially his wife, Josephine, were there when I needed them most.

I am also grateful to all the patrons who supported me through my years as a cosmetologist and shared their experiences with me. We learned from each other and grew better for it. I am thankful to my art collectors (named elsewhere in this book) and my teacher, Sr. Mary Ignatius Denay, who always encouraged and promoted my creativity.

And last but not least, I cannot imagine my life without my children: Miriam and her husband Christopher; Elizabeth and her husband, Bruce; Renee and her husband Mark. They have made the greatest contribution to my life and my story. (A special thanks to Elizabeth for typing out my manuscript and helping me put my story on paper).

I thank my grandchildren, who are my inspiration and also made contributions to this book through their experiences.

I give special recognition to Denise Crittendon, a kindred spirit, who shares my vision and helped with the writing and editing of this book.

Everyone who enriched my life has lead me to this moment in fulfilling my dream of writing and sharing my life lessons. To all of you, I offer my story and my humble thanks.